HIDDEN HISTORY
of
YOUNGSTOWN
and the
MAHONING VALLEY

Sean T. Posey

THE
History
PRESS

Published by The History Press
Charleston, SC
www.historypress.com

Front cover: Courtesy of the National Archives and Records Administration.
Back cover: Courtesy of Timothy Sokoloff.

First published 2022

ISBN 9781540251114

Library of Congress Control Number: 2021949222

Notice: The information in this book is true and complete to the best of our knowledge. It is offered without guarantee on the part of the author or The History Press. The author and The History Press disclaim all liability in connection with the use of this book.

*This book is dedicated to my parents, Fred and Kathleen,
and my uncle, Bryan Ridder.*

Contents

Acknowledgements

During the course of writing a book such as this, one accumulates debts. I would like to thank my parents for all their love and support. A special word of thanks goes to my uncle Bryan "Dew" Ridder for his ongoing support. Many thanks to the librarians and resources of the Mahoning and Trumbull County Library. The Canfield Historical Society was kind enough to provide access to their resources and photographs. Thomas Molocea and Historic Images have my eternal thanks for the many wonderful photographs contained in this book. I extend a special thanks to Timothy Sokoloff for access to his archives. He has always been gracious with his time and attention. I am also in the debt of Mark Peyko for his kind attention and encouragement during the writing of this book.

The following individuals were kind enough to share their memories, knowledge and resources: Stacey Adger, Bennie Allison, Don Attenberger, Bill DeCicco, Silverio Caggiano, Ron Flaviano, Vince Guerrieri, Shedrick Hobbs, Ken and Pam Krantz, Bill Lawson, Al Leonhart, Theresa Lyons, Mark Peyko, Tim Sokoloff, Barbara Stevens and Bill Umbel.

OUT OF THE PAST

F or many decades, the Mahoning Valley was known in the American
imagination as the Steel Valley. The mills lining the Mahoning River
served as smoky testaments to American industrial might itself,
which proved to be preeminent in the postwar world. During the 1950s, as
Youngstown celebrated its sesquicentennial, a travelogue produced by Carl
Dudley entitled *This Land of Ours* celebrated Youngstown as "one of the
most productive" metro areas "in the entire world." Indeed, Youngstown in
the 1950s represented one part of the "eight that make Ohio great," that is,
one of the eight larger cities that made the Buckeye State one of the most
important in the union.

In living memory, this is about as far back as most current and former
residents can remember. Some of the essays in this book cover history that
extends back into the late nineteenth and early twentieth centuries, a time
before the towering steel mills and the skyscrapers of downtown came to
dominate the landscape; a period when hitching posts, not parking spaces,
lined West Federal Street; a period when men wore high starched collars and
women's hatpins kept their purchases from the local millinery in place.

In the 1930s, the *Youngstown Vindicator* referred to the beginning of the
twentieth century as the dawning of "modern Youngstown." The first three
decades that followed are a key part of this book. Those decades were marked
by extreme inequality, increased immigration and incredibly violent labor
conflicts that rocked the valley and the country to its very core. The second
decade of the century, called "the violent 1910s" or the "violent teens" by

cultural evolutionist Peter Turchin, is the setting for the chapters on the fierce strikes of 1916 and 1919, along with the chapter on the emergence of the historic Youngstown Sheet and Tube company homes in what is now Campbell. Other Progressive Era experiments emerged during these years as well, including the genesis of a library branch for working people on Central Square. The traumatic experience of the Spanish flu pandemic, which has a new resonance today, put the entire valley and indeed much of the world under a black cloud. It too emerged during this period. These chapters are a glimpse into the history of the Mahoning Valley during an era of tremendous instability and rapid change. Today, most readers will likely be only dimly aware of this part of the valley's (and the nation's) history.

The trend of high levels of violence and inequity in American cities like Youngstown began to decline markedly during and after the 1930s, giving birth to a more stable and prosperous period of American history. This is often a period that economists and historians refer to as the "Great Compression," one in which many readers likely were born into. That evolution provides a backdrop to the events that make up the chapters on the Works Progress Administration. It is important to address this, because local history does not stand in isolation. At its best, local history can connect the history of a place or a region to wider trends in a country's history or even world history. I hope this is something the reader will keep in mind as they read through certain sections of the book.

The title of this book promises the reader a glimpse into the "hidden history" of our area, and that is worth commenting on. What is often referred to as hidden history is simply forgotten history. Events that my grandfather knew well are now almost entirely unknown to contemporary residents. Even more recent events, while perhaps easily recalled by older residents, are often totally unknown or "hidden" to those of the younger generations—for example, the history of the show *Route 66* (or indeed of the once-important Route 66 highway itself, something few in the millennial generation are likely to know much about it). The story of the Mahoning County Infirmary, an institution often shrouded in mystery, is emblematic of this idea. Even today, the fate of the many people buried on infirmary grounds is a story that has yet to be fully brought to light.

Perhaps no chapter in the book will represent the nature of hidden history in this area more than the story of how the *Negro Motorist Green Book* worked in Youngstown. The reality and nature of racial segregation in the Mahoning Valley is likely to be an uncomfortable one for many readers. However, Youngstown's experience with segregation is entirely representative of the

Laborers build a house in North Heights in 1914. Youngstown experienced rapid growth in population, labor conflict, crime and inequality during the "violent 1910s." *Courtesy of Thomas Molocea.*

larger industrial North itself during the early and mid-twentieth century. In her award-winning book on race in America, *Caste,* Isabel Wilkerson uses a particular painful story regarding the racially segregated public pool system in Youngstown to illustrate that larger history. The story of how the *Green Book* helped African American travelers navigate this environment in Youngstown is a micro history of that time in American history.

Whatever your age or individual experience with the Mahoning Valley, I hope these chapters will illuminate certain corridors of history for you. For today, much of our older industrial cities has been wiped away by economic collapse, disinvestment and migration away from the valley. With these developments has come an erosion of knowledge about this area's history. It is left to the local historian and, indeed, to the interest of readers, to help preserve the history of a part of the country that has played an outsized role in the evolution of America.

I

When the Spanish Flu Hung like a Black Cloud over the Mahoning Valley

Theaters, cafés, bars and churches closed. A deserted downtown Youngstown with hardly a soul on the street. An order for citizens to stay cloistered in their homes. This could have easily described the Youngstown area in the spring of 2020, but it is a description of the city over one hundred years ago as the Spanish flu hung like a black cloud over the Mahoning Valley and the world. "Pleasures were abandoned, even the most ordinary social amenities were almost foregone," wrote industrialist Joseph Butler in his 1921 book *History of Youngstown and the Mahoning Valley, Ohio*.

No one from his generation would forget the months of horror in the late fall and winter of 1918. However, until recently, the Spanish influenza was part of a "collective forgetting," according to Laura Spinney, author of *Pale Rider: The Spanish Flu of 1918 and How It Changed the World*. The same could be said here in the Mahoning Valley. For the story of the virus in this area is not just a part of local history. It holds lessons for those of us who have lived through COVID-19 and who are likely to face future pandemics.

The first documented cases in the United States of what became known as the Spanish influenza emerged in and around Camp Funston at Fort Riley in Kansas in March 1918. Soldiers' reports of sore throat, fever and headache proliferated. Hundreds fell ill at the base in the following weeks. Funston funneled rural conscripts into the American Expeditionary Force headed for France, helping to spread the virus. This was the first (comparatively mild) wave of the flu, one that had its biggest impact on the battlefields of Europe, slowing the German *Kaiserschlacht* offensive on the western front in

The northern corner of Central Square, circa 1918. *Courtesy of Thomas Molocea.*

the spring. Unlike the Allied and Central powers, which censored reporting, neutral Spain freely reported on the outbreak of influenza. This led to the initial impression that the virus, which became known as the Spanish flu or "grippe," had originated in Spain.

After dissipating during the summer, the virus emerged in Boston in August, bringing a wave of suffering that slowly unfolded during the fall and early winter. Most of the virus's victims (anywhere from 2.5 to 5 percent of the world's population) died between mid-September and mid-December, according to Spinney. Reporting in the *Youngstown Vindicator* estimated a death rate of between 7 and 10 percent for Ohio during the height of the outbreak.

On October 1, the *Chillicothe Gazette* reported that 60 percent of the city's population located near Camp Sherman, where influenza raged, was infected. On October 5, health authorities estimated there were between fifteen thousand and twenty thousand cases of influenza in the state. Authorities in Cincinnati issued a citywide ban on public gatherings that same day. One day later, the local Czecho-Slovak community held a rally in downtown Youngstown, attracting thousands of onlookers. A large gathering held at the South High School auditorium followed. This event almost certainly facilitated the spread of flu throughout the community. Three days later, the *Vindicator* called the outbreak of influenza in the area an "epidemic unchecked." Four deaths were reported along with twenty cases at the Glenwood Children's Home for a total of seventy-one new cases in one day. At the time of the parade, the local health board had reported only sixteen total cases in Youngstown. An October 7 editorial in the *Vindicator* offered only this advice to the area's residents: "At such a time as this, the thing to do is avoid exposure, take exercise, be moderate in living, get fresh air, and most of all don't become alarmed."

People did soon become alarmed. The *Youngstown Telegram* reported a total of 236 cases as of October 11. That same day, the board of health announced the closing of all churches, theaters, saloons, banquets, indoor gatherings, dance halls, poolrooms and bowling alleys. It urged streetcars to run below full capacity, and the police descended on East Federal Street to try to close coffeehouses and saloons that repeatedly refused to heed the order. On October 14, the board of health reported 850 cases and 11 total deaths. Hotels, where many railroad men and itinerant workers lived, remained open. "The only bright spots downtown were the hotel lobbies," the *Vindicator* reported. "Traveling men and others living in the hostelries, having no other places to go, thronged the corridors and lounging rooms, chatting, reading, or smoking. 'How long do you think this will last?' was the question asked by them all."

It did not take long for the hospital system to be overwhelmed. At the time, only Youngstown Hospital Association's facility on Oak Hill and St. Elizabeth's Hospital on Belmont served the city. Due to a marked lack of hospital beds, South High School and Jefferson Elementary School quickly transformed into emergency hospitals. Baldwin Memorial Kindergarten downtown became an influenza-maternity ward. Many professional nurses were in Europe as part of the war effort, and the local Red Cross, which helped lead the charge against the virus in the valley, estimated that the city lacked even a quarter of the nursing staff necessary to address the crisis. Much like what happened in New York City in the spring of 2020, hospitals in Youngstown and around the country urged nurses to graduate early and work in emergency facilities. Graduate nurses could expect to make $1.50 an hour (the equivalent of over $25.00 an hour in 2021 dollars), undergraduates $1.25 and nurse's aides $1.00.

Clergy, teachers and even students volunteered to work in the hospitals. One of the only firsthand accounts we have of that experience comes from Joseph Higley Jr., a student at the time, who told his tale to the Youngstown

South High was one of several schools that became makeshift hospitals during the pandemic. *Courtesy of the author.*

State Oral History Program in 1977. "We received the first patient, who was brought in with a dying condition," Higley told the interviewer. "They had one nurse on night duty. This first patient died. I had the preliminary job of laying him out, washing him and calling the undertaker." He estimated that about 90 of the approximately 380 patients at Jefferson Elementary School, where he volunteered, died. At South High School, three teachers who volunteered to nurse terminally ill patients succumbed to the flu. "Not one of us boys got even a sniffle from the flu, and yet people were dying all around us," Higley remembered.

The boys were lucky. Six-year-old Celia Krautheim died at South High only days after her mother, Catherine, and ten-year-old brother, Emil. Several officers who survived the war in Europe succumbed at home from flu-related pneumonia. Even Fred S. Bunn, the superintendent of Youngstown City Hospital, died while sick with influenza. The *Vindicator* reported twenty-nine deaths on October 29 alone—the height of the epidemic. The names of the dead and their addresses appeared daily in the paper like a grim mantra. No section of the city remained untouched. "Very few homes have escaped from the disease," the *Vindicator* reported of the Science Hill neighborhood, "and in some instances whole families are affected." By November 1, South High alone held nearly two hundred patients, five of

16

whom died that day. "Youngstown's population was roughly double what it is today," said Bill Lawson, head of the Mahoning Valley Historical Society. "The neighborhoods were very compact at that time; living conditions were tight. Large families and multiple families in dwellings." This proved to be a perfect environment for spreading the flu.

The flu spread quickly to Girard. By October 14, officials reported fifty active cases with "new cases being reported every few hours," according to the *Vindicator*. Girard's city fathers called on volunteers to emulate the wartime courage of their "brothers in khaki" and serve in the local emergency hospital. Schools in Lowellville closed on October 14, and Sharon Steel Hoop turned its clubhouse over to the village for use as a hospital. One Lowellville resident lost twelve family members to the flu. Local quarantine regulations prohibited him from attending their funerals. In East Palestine, with a population of approximately five thousand , twelve flu patients died in one week in early October. "People are forbidden to call on neighbors," the *Vindicator* reported. "Every form of social entertainment, lodge meetings and civic and church societies are forbidden." Statewide, the *Cincinnati Enquirer* reported 100,000 flu-related cases on October 21.

Custodian Earl O. Van Kirk volunteered to serve as an orderly at the South High emergency hospital during the darkest days of the pandemic. He, too, contracted influenza and died in early November. Several teachers who volunteered as orderlies also died while serving at South High. *Photo by the author.*

Local historian Florence Galida described how the flu ravaged East Youngstown: "Those who died were buried as soon as coffins were available. There was activity in every cemetery, every day until the peak was passed. Many remember the horse-drawn wagons trudging up the hills to the cemeteries and the burials every day in the St. Nicholas cemetery on Hyatt Avenue, many in graves which were never to have a headstone."

Desperate citizens turned to patent medicines, a common scourge of the era, to ward off influenza. Ads for Hyomei inhalers, basically an antiseptic inhaler containing eucalyptus and advertised as a flu preventative, appeared regularly in the *Vindicator*. People also melted camphor with lard and rubbed it over their throats, an old-fashioned method of supposedly warding off the flu. Influenza-inspired poetry was printed in the paper. This poem appeared in the *Toledo Blade*:

> *I wish the flu would fly by night*
> *and all the germs might freeze.*
> *It fills my nights with dread and fright*
> *to snort and sniff and sneeze....*

The outbreaks of influenza appeared to subside in the city in early November. During a tour of the area, Dr. J.E. Hunter of the U.S. Public Health Service said, "Youngstown is the best organized, in the best shape to handle the epidemic of any city in the state." South High reported 5 deaths on November 5, the lowest number in days. Yet any jubilation appeared premature, as the *Vindicator* reported 233 new cases and 27 deaths on November 8. In the city of Warren, the flu ban was lifted on December 15. As of December 21, Youngstown officials continued to limit capacity at both saloons and theaters. By that time, Youngstown's health department had reported 9,858 cases of influenza and 779 deaths. Seven days later, the city lifted the remaining restrictions on businesses and public gatherings.

Youngstown in the early 1900s was plagued by incredibly high crime rates, according to the research of journalist Joe Gorman. In 1915, approximately 14,618 people found themselves arrested in the city, at a time when the population approached 130,000. As the flu began to dissipate, a new crime wave hit beleaguered Youngstown, which the *Telegram* in turn blamed (perhaps rightly) on chaos caused by the pandemic. The headline "Thugs Unchecked in Vice Carnival" dominated the front page as the year's end drew near. The *Telegram* darkly joked that perhaps a "flu ban on local holdups" should be proposed. Yet the worst of the pandemic seemed to

Red Cross flags decorate West Federal Street in spring 1919. The organization helped recruit hospital workers in response to the valley's influenza outbreak. *Courtesy of the National Archives and Records Administration.*

be over. The flu, however, did not disappear altogether. "In December, as contaminated soldiers returned to America in the cramped quarters of ships, the third wave began," writes historian Ann Hagedorn. On December 17, Niles postmaster James Paul Stewart died from complications of influenza, and obituaries for flu victims continued to appear in the daily papers.

On January 11, 1919, the *Vindicator* reported twenty-six new flu cases, an increase from the previous day. Three days later, the paper reported seven deaths and thirty-five new cases of the flu, an increase of five deaths from the previous day. On January 19, a man from Pittsburgh was immediately removed from a B&O train car in Youngstown after exhibiting signs of the flu. "The public must be careful to avoid a second epidemic. Easier to prevent than cure," read a notice in the *Vindicator* on January 13. In October 1919, one year after Spanish flu came to the valley, state health officials reported that the epidemic had dissipated in Ohio. "Cases are few and scattered," state news services reported.

Local officials, however, could not agree on how successful the shutdowns had been in controlling the virus. An editorial in the *Telegram* argued that the so-called public quarantine had failed to do much and in any case could not be adopted as "a permanent policy," though it had never been advertised as such. Members of the school board blamed the pubic for failing to follow recommended guidelines.

Interventions such as "social distancing" (a term not used during the time of Spanish flu) and bans on large public gatherings did, however, make a difference in the impact of the virus. This is one of the conclusions the National Academy of Sciences came to in a 2007 paper examining the response of various municipalities to the Spanish flu: "Cities in which multiple interventions were implemented at an early phase of the epidemic had peak death rates ≈ (approximately equal to) 50% lower than those that did not and had less-steep epidemic curves."

Youngstown and in particular nearby Pittsburgh fared poorly during the pandemic, according to the University of Michigan Medical School's Influenza Encyclopedia. Among "large cities," Youngstown finished with seventh-highest death rate in 1918 and second highest in the nation in 1919. Pittsburgh had the highest death rate in 1919 and the second highest in 1918. The Czecho-Slovak parade in early October helped spread influenza throughout the Youngstown area. Similarly, in Philadelphia, the Liberty Loan Parade held on September 28 attracted an estimated 200,000 people. Within days, over 600 cases emerged, and approximately 16,000 Philadelphians died over the next six months.

In the years that followed, the pandemic faded from local (and national) memory. A post-pandemic depression in 1920–21, Prohibition, women's suffrage, the Roaring Twenties and a host of other concerns occupied an ever-changing nation. It would not be until over a century later, with the emergence of COVID-19, that the Mahoning Valley and the nation would be fully reminded of the dark days of the Spanish flu.

2

Steel Valley Sluggers

An Early History of Youngstown Baseball

D uring the warm summer months, you can be sure to find families pulling into the parking lot at Eastwood Field in Niles, ready to enjoy another night of baseball courtesy of the Mahoning Valley Scrappers. Since 1999, the Scrappers have represented the valley. However, unbeknownst to most of the fans, the history of Mahoning Valley baseball stretches back well before even 1899. Over the decades, a bevy of teams, leagues, fields and ballplayers have made the area one of the most exciting places in the nation to watch minor league, amateur and sandlot baseball.

In the years after the Civil War, baseball surpassed the English game of cricket to become the most popular sport in America, according to historian Douglas E. Bukowski. "Recent arrivals in the cities from the nation's small towns and farms found escape from the hurly-burly of urban life in bucolic baseball stadiums, small islands of greenery surrounded by acres of concrete." As Youngstown began to increasingly industrialize, the first baseball fields to emerge in the 1880s and '90s were modest affairs. A place called "The Flats" was one of the first. Young men congregated at a field not far from West Federal Street at the corner of Gardner Street and North Ardale—an area since transformed beyond recognition by urban renewal. Hazen Park, named for Charles Hazen, an early Youngstown baseball manager, later hosted teams near Mosier Road in Girard, near the future site of the Ohio Oil Cloth Company.

From the beginning, notable players emerged from Youngstown. Jimmy McAleer, born in 1864, grew up on the west side of the city and graduated from Rayen. He began playing local baseball in 1882 before eventually heading to South Carolina to play ball. McAleer became part owner of a touring comedy troupe based in Youngstown while he was a player. He eventually made his way into the majors, playing for the Cleveland Spiders. His name was advanced as a potential candidate for mayor of Youngstown in 1895, such was his popularity in the Mahoning Valley. During his prime, he was considered one of the best center fielders in the game. McAleer eventually quit playing in the late 1890s and headed back to Youngstown to run a downtown haberdashery.

McAleer returned to the game in a dual role as a player-manager for the Cleveland Lake Shores, a precursor to the Cleveland Indians. However, he was destined to play a bigger historical role in baseball, helping Ban Johnson develop the St. Louis Browns in the emerging American League. McAleer, a friend of Johnson's, proved pivotal in recruiting players for the nascent league. McAleer helped friends from Youngstown, as well. According to his biographer, David Strickler, the career of John D. "Bonesetter" Reese took off after McAleer vouched for his talents at treating injured ballplayers. Reese went on to become famous, working with everyone from Honus Wagner to Cy Young and Ty Cobb.

After years as a manager for various teams, he eventually became club president of the 1912 World Series champion Boston Red Sox. After their victory, McAleer returned to Youngstown as a hero. The *Vindicator* described a raucous parade on the day of his homecoming. "As the auto bearing Mr. McAleer turned into West Federal Street, hundreds of sticks of red fire were burning at Central Square, while the quiet atmosphere was occasionally punctured by the explosion of a bomb." The turnout and the attention paid to McAleer made an impression on the paper, which claimed that "never before in Youngstown history had such a demonstration been tendered to any one man."

When McAleer began playing in the early 1880s, the game had yet to capture the imagination of Youngstowners, according to baseball historian Rich Blevins. Historian Richard Worth states that the local baseball team even lacked a name. According to historians Craig Holbert and Margaret and Thomas Maroon, "It was not uncommon to have teams known by the area as opposed to having a team nickname." Still, most Youngstowners paid more attention to the local cycling scene than they did to baseball.

In general, tracking the earliest baseball teams and their rosters is difficult. "There was a certain fluidity as to what constituted professional baseball," journalist and baseball historian Vince Guerrieri explained. "Up until the twenties or thirties, the idea of what we now know of as the minor league farm system didn't exist. There were these independent teams that would make their money from the gate and when they sold the contracts of their players to major league teams or higher-level minor-league teams. There were plenty of teams that would just sprout up, and leagues that would just sprout up and play for a little while and then kind of fade into oblivion."

The Youngstown Giants (sometimes called the "Little Giants") was one of the first teams to gain notice in the Interstate League before fading into obscurity. The city had more success with the Youngstown Ohio Works, which played in the Ohio and Pennsylvania League. Backed by local steel-industry icons Joseph and Thomas McDonald, the team captured the league championship in 1905 and 1906. The often-rowdy home games were played at South Side Stadium at the corner of Hillman Street and Warren Avenue. A few future major leaguers also made their way onto the Ohio Works squad. Bill Phyle, who went on to start with several teams in the majors, played for the team. Future big-leaguer Roy Castleton played on the 1906 championship team. He drew comparisons to Cy Young (who had played years earlier for a team in Canton) after he pitched a perfect game against Akron.

The Ohio Works team helped start the career of Hall of Famer Billy Evans. Having grown up on the north side of Youngstown, Evans (who was in the same class at Rayen as Albert Warner of the Warner brothers) became a sports reporter and eventually sports editor for the *Vindicator.* While covering an Ohio Works game in Homestead, Pennsylvania, Evans improbably was asked to step into the game after the designated umpire failed to show. He continued to work for a time as both an umpire and a reporter. In 1906, he made the transition to the major leagues, becoming, at twenty-two, the youngest umpire in major league history. Evans later became the youngest umpire to officiate in a World Series.

In 1907, another first-class ballfield emerged, and the Ohio Works team came to an end. In May, Willis Park, originally planned for the corner of Glenwood and Parkview Avenues, opened on the corner of Glenwood and Grace Avenues, which is now Sherwood. The Youngstown Champs became the next team to hit the baseball diamond in the Ohio and Pennsylvania League at Willis Park. The Champs became league champions in 1907 before becoming defunct the very next season—such was the nature of minor-league baseball at the time.

Baseball came to play a big role in "Americanizing" newcomers to the burgeoning industrial city. As the years passed, immigrant communities in Youngstown only grew. With that growth came tension between the older Anglo Protestant culture and the new arrivals. Youngstown's burgeoning manufacturing concerns also feared that immigrants were insufficiently Americanized, as well as perhaps carriers of what they considered to be dangerous ideas such as syndicalism and trade unionism. According to Sherry Linkon and John Russo, companies responded in part by pursuing "open-shop" policies such as the "American plan" and "welfare capitalism." These policies led companies to "developments such as worker housing, company newspapers, company-sponsored sports teams, and other leisure activities."

Youngstown Sheet and Tube eventually transformed an old slag pile into Campbell Field (which was in Struthers). Baseball games and company outings were usually held at the park. Proceeds from the company-sponsored dances at Campbell Park flowed to the company team, which played in the City Federation League. Other companies also fielded their own teams. Republic Rubber, which had a large clubhouse for employees and a baseball diamond on Albert Street, fielded a team. General Fireproofing built a diamond for employees at the corner of Gypsy Lane off Logan Avenue.

Ethnic baseball organizations such as the Slovak League emerged as well, becoming especially popular in places like Campbell during the Depression. "They had the Hungarians and the Slovak league," Campbell resident Billy Kish later recalled. "They used to play up on top the hill by the water tank, up across Struthers Liberty Road....It was all empty there. There were a couple ballparks. We always went up there to watch ball games."

Teams with names like the Struthers Slovaks, the Haselton Dodgers and the Wooden Shoes Beers battled one another. The first boys' leagues came together in the early 1900s, bringing the Victors, the Silver Tops, the Red Stars and others onto fields across the city. Large entertainment venues had their own diamonds, too. The Southern Park Trotting Track in Boardman had a field and team in the early 1900s. And, of course, Idora Park's field saw lots of action in the 1940s. The sport quickly spread to high schools around the valley, bringing in new generations of fans and players.

By the early 1920s, according to author Craig Lammers, "Youngstown no longer had the resources or talent to compete with the top independent teams." In the late teens, football at Wright Field overshadowed the baseball games held there. Wright Field was home to the Youngstown Patricians, a semiprofessional football team that laid claim to the pre-NFL football championship in 1915. Minor-league ball returned to prominence during the early years of the Great Depression. Two Mid-Atlantic League teams played at Idora in the early 1930s, but they quickly came and went. In 1939, the Youngstown Browns, the farm team for the St. Louis Browns, began playing at Idora. The *Vindicator* reacted to the announcement with less than

Members of the Republic Rubber baseball team pose for a portrait, 1906. *Courtesy of Thomas Molocea.*

Members of the Brier Hill baseball team pose for a portrait, 1906. *Courtesy of Thomas Molocea.*

The 1931 Wilson High baseball team, one of many popular school teams in the valley. *Courtesy of Thomas Molocea.*

marked enthusiasm: "The old teams that played at Willis Park out on the South Side and later at Wright Field were outgrowths of genuine local demand. The club coming here now was tossed our way because the St. Louis Browns need a farm [team], and there doesn't seem to be any better place to put this particular item of it."

Youngstowners did, however, have a chance to watch players from the big leagues at Idora. Players "barnstorming" through Youngstown gave the locals a chance to see some of the biggest names in the game on the diamond right here in the city. "Barnstorming was a big deal," Guerrieri said. "And not just because people would be able to see major league players in person that they normally wouldn't be able to see, but it was also a legitimate source of income for major leaguers as well. It's only been effectively in our lifetimes that players have been as highly paid as they are." Some of the big leaguers fans saw included Whitey Ford, Walter Alston, Frank McCormick, Floyd Baker, Vern Stephens, Joe Page, Mel Queen, Ed Stanky, Joe Beggs, Wally Westlake and many others.

Top players from the Negro Leagues barnstormed through the valley as well, and Youngstown produced players who made their way onto African

American baseball teams. Claude "Hooks" Johnson played for a variety of teams during his career from 1916 to 1930. He got his start as an athlete playing basketball, football and track for South High and Rayen. He died in Youngstown in 1965 and is buried in Tod Cemetery. In his obituary in the *Vindicator*, Johnson was described as a player who likely would have been a star in the major leagues if baseball had been integrated during his career. W. James Cobbin graduated from North High School in 1953 and played for the New York Black Yankees and the Indianapolis Clowns before getting drafted. He lives and works in Youngstown and is the vice-president of Yesterday's Negro League Baseball Players Foundation, which aims to honor the legacy of his fellow players.

Theodore R. "Terrible Ted" Page, originally from Kentucky, spent his youth in Monkey's Nest, where he became a standout athlete. In *Voices from the Great Black Baseball Leagues*, Page recalled playing baseball at the Booker T. Washington Settlement on West Federal Street. "We had a little clubhouse there," he said. "Used to come from my neighborhood, Monkey's Nest." He played with several teams over his career, including the Homestead Grays. During the depths of the Depression, Page barnstormed across the country with some of the top Black players, including the famed Satchel Paige.

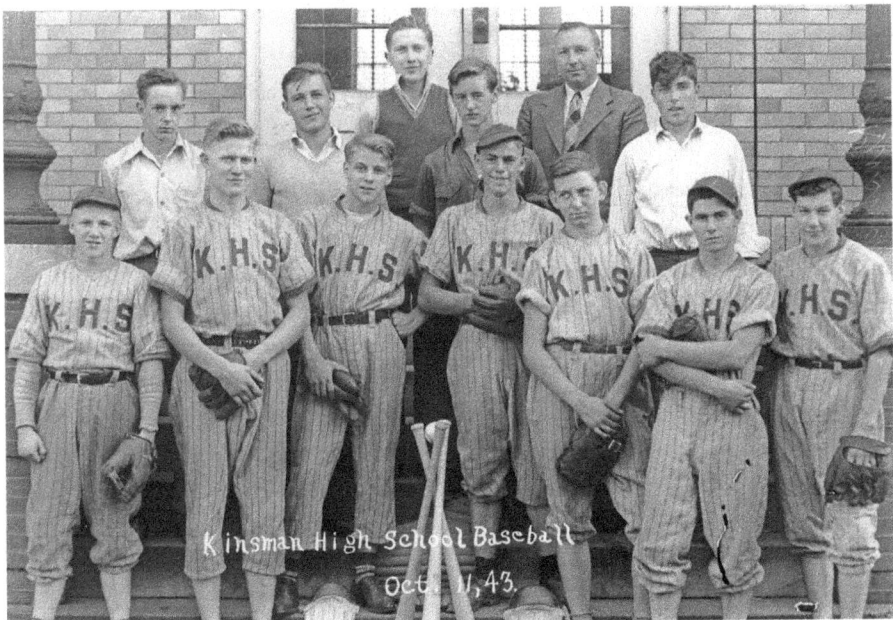

The 1943 Kinsman High School baseball team. *Courtesy of Thomas Molocea.*

Above: Over the years, myriad great amateur and professional baseball players graced the diamond at Idora Park. *Courtesy of Thomas Molocea.*

Opposite: The crumbling stands of the abandoned Stambaugh Field as they appeared in 2012. *Photo by the author.*

After the interruptions of World War II, Mid-Atlantic League Baseball returned to Idora with the Youngstown Gremlins. However, minor-league baseball in general began to decline in the postwar era. During the 1950s, fans could watch Major League Baseball on television in the comfort of their own homes, which greatly impacted the demand for minor-league teams. Beyond that, minor-league ball teams at Idora had to compete with the extraordinary baseball one could see being played at the many other fields in the city, according to Guerrieri. "One of the problems was that the field at Idora Park wasn't as nice as Pemberton or any of the other fields. There was such vibrant amateur baseball; it basically crowded out the minor league scene. The teams in Youngstown were Class D, and they don't even go down to Class D anymore in the minors."

In 1944, Youngstown hosted the thirty-second-annual National Amateur Baseball Federation Championship. It was the fourth time the city hosted

28

the prestigious all-amateur event. One reason for selecting Youngstown was the city's baseball fields, which the *New York Times* referred to as some "of the finest sandlot diamonds in the country." This was the case well into the 1950s, according to Bill DeCicco, who grew up watching and playing baseball in the valley. "You had teams coming from all over the United States to play tournaments in Youngstown." Youngstown possessed plenty of quality ballfields, including Ipe, Oakland, Gibson, Pemberton, Nick Johnson (also known as Bailey), Evans, Borts, Tod, Stambaugh and Victory. This proved true deep into the 1970s, when slow-pitch, Babe Ruth, Little League and PONY activities kept the city's well-maintained fields full every summer. However, the closing of the steel mills and the subsequent depopulation of the city's neighborhoods (and coffers) helped put an end to many of the old ball fields in the city.

The nature of the game changed, too, Guerrieri said. "Baseball is now in a lot of ways an upper-class sport. It's for people who can afford the latest equipment; who can afford to be on a travel team; who can afford to do all these things that get you noticed. So, you can if you want to, play in high school and beyond." Yet every year you can find the boys of summer out on the local diamonds. Millcreek Junior Baseball, Boardman Community Baseball, Austintown Girls Softball League, the Ohio Glaciers, the Scrappers, and others continue to carry on a tradition in Youngstown that dates to the days of Rutherford B. Hayes.

3

THE HIDDEN HISTORY OF
THE MAHONING COUNTY INFIRMARY

I f you drive west down Herbert Road in Canfield, and if you have a good eye, you will notice a little WPA-built bridge to nowhere on your right. Situated to the north, it leads across Sawmill Creek. At its end, an old, forlorn-looking gate still creaks in the breeze. Beyond are only trees and thickets—and farther back, homes. Until 1968, this gate led to the Mahoning County Infirmary complex. Known by locals as the "Pogey" and later referred to as the Mahoning County Home (or simply the "Home") after a 1919 change required that the "infirmary" designation be officially changed to "home." The infirmary housed the county's indigent population: "hobos," the "down on their luck," the aged and the disabled. At various times, it also housed tuberculosis patients and the mentally ill. Kids were born and lived at the infirmary. The bodies of some of these men, women and children are still interred in the old grounds, which is now the site of an environmentally protected easement and housing developments.

The origin of the poorhouse (or almshouse) in America dates to New England in the mid-1600s. However, according to Lucy Komisar, these institutions did not become common until the 1800s, due to the "sparsely settled" nature of America up to that point. That soon changed. According to historian Michael B. Katz, "Throughout the century before the New Deal, the poorhouse dominated the structure of welfare—or, as it was called then, relief. Although despised, dreaded, and often attacked, the poorhouse endured as the central arch of public welfare policy." In short,

The old infirmary gate is one of the few visible reminders of the facility that dominated Herbert Road for over a century. *Photo by the author.*

the Mahoning County Infirmary and others like it served as a backstop for what were called society's "unfortunates" in an era before the advent of the modern welfare state.

Before the existence of the county infirmary, any public charge in Mahoning Valley was either cared for in their municipality or, as local researchers have documented, forcibly run out of town. Prior to the establishment of Mahoning County in 1846, some in the Youngstown area possibly were sent to the Trumbull County Poorhouse. (Prior to 1850, county infirmaries in Ohio were known as poorhouses.) The Mahoning County Infirmary was not originally intended to serve large numbers of what were called insane persons; however, despite many problems, a department for the mentally ill did emerge to house this population.

Researchers Wendell F. Lauth, Jennifer L. Neff and Patricia D. Wiant discovered that the original infirmary complex opened in November 1855. A brief description of the facility appeared in the *Republican Sentinel*: "The building is pleasantly located on a productive looking farm—is well built and well finished....Its exterior has a benevolent appearance generally, while its interior displays charitable features particularly, compelling the most common observer to feel proud of such institutions and of the

31

The newly rebuilt infirmary complex, opened in 1898, reflected a Victorian-era design. *Courtesy of the Canfield Historical Society.*

liberality of the people who willingly furnish the means to thus provide for unfortunate humanity."

Among some of the first occupants were Mrs. Daniel Duches, age sixty-five, listed as a "cripple"; Mary Randolph, seventy-five, listed as "infirm"; and Edward Hughes, a miner who "had a legal situation before insanity." A June 1857 article in the *Mahoning Register* states that the facility housed 26 inmates, 2 of whom were listed as "delirious." The article was one of the first to describe the facility's farm. Such institutions with working farms were often referred to colloquially as "poor farms." Infirmary farms in Ohio were perhaps most viewed as producing food for inmates of the facility and/ or for the commercial market. The neighboring infirmary in Columbiana County also featured a farm. At the time, wheat was grown on the grounds in Canfield. By 1880, the infirmary farm consisted of 190 acres of tilled land, 24 acres of grassland, 24 with hay and 40 acres of woodland. Horses, mules, cattle and pigs were on the farm by this point. That same year, the *Mahoning Dispatch* listed 90 paupers at the infirmary, most of them coming from Youngstown proper. There were 97 inmates (the commonly used term) listed in 1881 and 198 receiving outside relief.

The *Dispatch* regularly included coverage of the infirmary, especially when it concerned the annual report and the year's various expenditures for the facility. Editorials in the paper consistently criticized the policy of providing "outside relief" (as opposed to the "indoor relief" of the poorhouse). An 1878 editorial pointed to what it called the "large percentage" of relief going to indigent individuals outside of the infirmary's walls. "They [outside paupers] will not strive to do anything for themselves, but will remain in slothful idleness," the paper declared in 1878. This thinking may have developed from examples set elsewhere in America. According to historian David Wagner, it was policy in many counties that "poor people, including the elderly and children, were to be aided only at the poorhouse and not encouraged in 'pauperism' by outside relief." Systems of "outside relief" would not find widespread purchase until the era of the Great Depression and the New Deal.

As early as the 1840s, crusaders such as Dorothea Dix had advocated for the removal of the mentally ill from poorhouses. Yet the housing of the mentally ill in the Mahoning County Infirmary, which continued for decades, would be the source of much consternation during the institution's existence. A particularly disturbing article on the subject appeared in the *Dispatch* in 1882. Increasing numbers of mentally ill inmates were being housed in the infirmary at the time, and the facility did not appear to have the means to adequately accommodate them. The *Dispatch* described a Hadean scene in the "insane department" with inmates "so demented and wild in their actions" that they presented a constant challenge to the staff. A putrid smell engulfed much of the building, according to the paper, and inmates in the dining room received "the full benefit of the stench and foul gasses that arise every time the doors leading to the insane department are opened." This description seems to generally reflect the state's infirmaries as described in an 1869 report by the Ohio General Assembly, which referred to conditions in many of these institutions as "disgraceful" and "shameful." Many infirmaries did not have adequate facilities even for those not suffering from mental illnesses, and many counties in the state lacked an infirmary of any kind.

After expanding sleeping rooms for new inmates in the 1890s, the old infirmary complex came to a stark and sudden end on the night of February 20, 1897. What the *Youngstown Vindicator* described at the time as "one of the most disastrous fires that has ever visited Mahoning County" started in an air shaft shortly after lights out on a Saturday evening. It soon engulfed most of the complex. The infirmary superintendent and staff moved the

240 inmates out ahead of the flames. Amazingly enough, only 1 man, an inmate of the insane wing, died after rushing back into one of the burning buildings. County officials transferred the inmates to a variety of facilities, including the Park Hotel in Canfield, the county jail and the Columbiana and Portage County infirmaries. Residents of Canfield took in several of the older women while the new infirmary was planned and built.

The new infirmary, which opened in September 1898, proved to be a marked improvement over the former facility. With accommodations for hundreds of inmates (the superintendent and his family also lived on the grounds), the facility consisted of five buildings. The layout included an administration wing, a kitchen and laundry building and a boiler house. The women's building, which included an attached facility for the mentally ill, was located to the west of the men's building. The facility itself was in the shape of a triangle. The women's building contained a small chapel for religious services. Both the men's and women's dorms had small hospitals, and the infirmary came equipped with a morgue. After inspecting the new facility, J.P. Byers, secretary of the board of state charities, called the Canfield complex a "model county infirmary."

Just over a decade later, a fire destroyed the men's dormitory, claiming the lives of four inmates in early 1909. Another ten suffered severe burns. According to the *Vindicator*, one of the injured inmates, Dennis Mahoney, ended up "frightfully burned and he is almost helpless." Despite this fire also being of unknown origin, it is possible that the neglect of Superintendent Robert Taylor may have played a role. Two years earlier, a grand jury found that inmates at the infirmary had suffered abuse and neglect during Taylor's tenure and that the facility itself was dirty and inundated with vermin. Prosecutor W.R. Graham declined to pursue the investigation, saying that he would leave the grand jury's report for the infirmary's directors to sort out. However, for whatever reason, they did not act, and Taylor remained at the helm. At this time, was the facility still "one of the finest infirmaries in the state," as the *Weekly Guernsey Times* in Cambridge claimed? It is not clear.

In the early 1900s, the infirmary also housed a portion of the county's tuberculosis patients. Often known as consumption, the "white plague" of tuberculosis represented one of the leading causes of death at the time. In the late nineteenth century, sanitoriums (often located away from urban areas) to house and treat the ill in seclusion began to open. For a time, patients in Mahoning County were treated at a tuberculosis hospital on the infirmary grounds. The facility was separated from the rest of the complex, and two nurses served the approximately twenty-two available beds. When case

Exterior of the infirmary. *Courtesy of the Canfield Historical Society.*

levels increased, county officials erected tents to accommodate new patients. This hospital was closed in 1915, and the patients, some near death, were transferred to the Springfield Lake Sanitarium near Cleveland.

A 1926 investigation of Ohio infirmaries reported by the *Vindicator* found inmates in Canfield "well taken care of." At the time, no mentally ill patients were reported on the premises. Most of the inmates consisted of those over the age of sixty, including some suffering from dementia. The reporter made special note of epileptics who could not find room at the Ohio Hospital for Epileptics in Gallipolis. However, there were not adequate facilities for treating them at the infirmary.

Conditions changed enormously in the 1930s. The catastrophic Depression years, especially the early 1930s, when unemployment in America peaked, put a severe strain on the infirmary and its resources. In 1925, approximately 172 men and women were housed in the facility. That number had increased to 290 by January 1930 and again to almost 300 in late 1932. A 1933 article in the *Dispatch* described how several bedraggled men found food and shelter at Canfield town hall after finding no available lodging at the infirmary. According to the *Youngstown Telegram*, "Efforts to keep the number of men housed at the infirmary down to the capacity already reached are nearly

A postcard depicts the administration building and the men's wing of the infirmary. *Courtesy of the author.*

overcome by the large number of 'drifters,' who arrive almost daily seeking a night's lodging and food." These were men who had to have walked many miles from Youngstown, where they reported finding no available room at the city's "flophouse." Mahoning ranked sixth among Ohio counties for the average number of inmates housed in the local infirmary in 1932, and as late as 1938, it housed 385 inmates, the *Telegram* reported.

In the wake of a calamitous fire that killed 322 men at the Ohio Penitentiary in 1930, county officials and *Telegram* reporter Arthur Todd inspected the Canfield complex and found very different circumstances from 1926. Much of the men's wing proved to be a firetrap. Old men were crammed into an attic chamber with only a narrow stairway to guide them to safety in case of a fire. In any event, many of them could hardly walk. The larger complex itself proved to be quite unpleasant, according to Todd. "In spite of the hospital-like cleanliness, a repulsive odor that permeates antiquated, poorly ventilated buildings oppresses one." However, the county commissioners, themselves aware of the financial challenges facing the infirmary, continued to support Superintendent Charles Lee.

The best resource in terms of firsthand accounts of the later decades of the infirmary's existence comes from the memoirs of Wade Schisler, whose uncle served as superintendent from 1916 to 1939. His father worked in the boiler house, and his mother worked in the dining hall and kitchen. Schisler recalled other employees of the institution, including Guy Musser, who lived on the infirmary farm and managed the cow barn. The forty Holstein dairy cattle he looked after produced the milk and butter for the entire facility. According to him, the inmates lined up every Wednesday outside of the milk house for their ration of buttermilk. Most of the able-bodied inmates had chores and worked in the infirmary's garden during the summer and fall.

Schisler spent a lot of time in the men's facility, which he described as a three-story building. It had no elevator, so men with mobility issues lived on the first floor. When his parents went away for day trips, he was allowed to spend time with the men, who often entertained him with stories of their lives before they came to the Pogey. According to him, some had been successful businessmen, professionals or tradesmen before falling on "hard times." Although there was a three-cell jail in the facility, it was apparently never used, Schisler suggested. "All of the men got along fine, and I never saw a fight, loud argument or even heard swearing." The men and women rarely fraternized, and he recalled that services in the chapel represented the only time when men were allowed in the women's dormitory. Only in the dining hall did the sexes mix.

An undated photo shows men gathered outside of the infirmary during the warmer months. *Courtesy of the Canfield Historical Society.*

Not everyone who came to the infirmary stayed indefinitely. Schisler vividly recalled one of the colorful characters who briefly visited the Pogey, a hitchhiker covered from head to toe in tattoos. The man told him he had formerly worked with a famous traveling circus, appearing as the "World's Most Tattooed Man": "Back then you, you didn't see people all decorated as you do today. He said he started drinking, and when he missed shows he got fired from the circus. Now he was just going from town to town working fairs and carnivals and doing anything to make a living. He stayed a couple of days, thanked us, waved goodbye and was gone up the road."

According to Schisler, the infirmary declined during its last years. Official reports and reporting in the *Vindicator* confirm that the infirmary was indeed in decline. Near the end of World War II, the Mahoning County Welfare Advisory Board issued a report on conditions at the home, which they called "a disgrace and an eyesore." The facility was chronically understaffed, the report noted, and there were cases of untrained personnel mixing medications for patients. At this point, the facilities in Canfield proved inferior to those found in other Ohio counties, the report stated.

In 1953, the Coordinating Council of the Community Corporation of Greater Youngstown recommended the infirmary facilities receive a complete overhaul and that the farm "play no more than an auxiliary role in the life of an institution whose first concern should be people." Additionally, the report linked the antiquated institution to an era "when there was a general belief that a community's poor or infirm could best be cared for out of sight of other people." It stated, "The Home now exists in a time of greatly changed attitudes." The report helped accelerate an ongoing discussion about relocating the facility entirely.

As the 1950s progressed, and as needed repairs and changes at the infirmary continued to mount, the Mahoning County Welfare Advisory Board recommended that a new facility be built at another location. In late 1959, after voters supported a levy to fund a new county home, the county commissioners passed a resolution to close the current facility and sell 280 acres of infirmary land. County commissioners permanently shuttered the aged infirmary on Herbert Road in 1962. Residents were relocated to a new facility, the Mahoning County Nursing Home on Kirk Road in Austintown. The old Victorian-era buildings off Herbert Road, frequently targeted by vandals, sat and decayed for several years. Arsonists destroyed most of the buildings in 1968, and the charred remains were soon unceremoniously demolished. This is perhaps where the history of the old infirmary should end, yet one chapter of its history remains open.

The infirmary's original cemetery was located between Sawmill Creek and Herbert Road. *Photo by the author.*

In the spring of 1857, the *Mahoning Register* reported a recent death among the inmates and stated that "the selection of a suitable burying ground may be worthy of the consideration of the board of directors." According to researcher Wendell F. Lauth, the deceased was likely James Haney, who probably was the first inmate buried on the infirmary grounds. It is unclear if his death marked the point when the original infirmary cemetery came into existence. The infirmary cemetery was established as the last option for deceased inmates whose remains were not claimed. Research done by Robert Aigler, a former member of the Mahoning County Chapter of the Ohio Genealogical Society, discovered that the original infirmary cemetery was located between Sawmill Creek and Herbert Road near the entrance to the infirmary itself. The original cemetery's location is also marked on the 1874 Mahoning County atlas map of Canfield.

The old cemetery land is now an environmentally protected area. Few headstones were likely ever erected, and none are visible today, though the remains of the cemetery's old rock wall can still be glimpsed. Whatever records existed for the original cemetery, including how many inmates are buried there (and are still in the ground), likely went up in flames in the 1897 fire. In his reminiscences about life at the infirmary, Wade Schisler wrote,

"My dad also told me of another place on the farm that a few people were buried, and I am probably the only one that knows about it. If they ever widen Herbert Road, someone may find a surprise when they start digging." This indicates that an unknown number of bodies could be buried on the old infirmary farm property.

Much more can be said about the second known infirmary cemetery. Long after the demolition of the infirmary buildings themselves in 1968, the burial ground north of the main complex remained. It is not known when exactly inmates began to be buried there, but this cemetery became the center of controversy in the 1980s and 1990s as development sprouted up around it. The only surviving records of infirmary deaths cover the years 1907 to 1946. During that time, approximately 1,650 inmates died, and at least 428 were buried on the infirmary grounds. Records complied by the Ohio Genealogical Society include the names of the deceased, their age at the time of death and whether they were buried in the infirmary cemetery. Instead of grave markers, the infirmary used round cylinders, referred to as tiles. Each tile had a number, which is linked in the register to the name of the person buried beneath it. Men, women, veterans (including from the Civil War) and even children were interred in the cemetery. For example, tile number 103 marked the grave of Dannie Tokes, a stillborn baby who was buried in June 1912.

Some of the stories of these individuals can be traced. Tile number 241 marked the grave of Charles Jackson, who was found ill in a barn in early 1918. According to the *Telegram*, he claimed to be a natural-born citizen "but either could not or would not" reveal anything about his earlier life. He died at the infirmary two months later and was buried. William Johnson, tile number 114, was an African American laborer who had come north from his native Georgia. He lived at 234 East Boardman in Street in Youngstown before becoming sick with tuberculosis. He died at the infirmary's tuberculosis hospital and was buried in the cemetery in March 1913.

A 1989 article in the *Vindicator*, "Past and Future of Cemeteries Pose Mystery," refers to "a cemetery with small, numbered markers and a meager wire fence." The property the burial ground was located on had just been purchased by Charlie Masters, treasurer of B&J Enterprises. "Our intention is to leave them there," Masters told the *Vindicator*. "I'm not into digging people up."

The *Vindicator* reported that the new owner claimed that only those who died during the Spanish flu were buried in the cemetery, which is not accurate. Almost a decade later, a housing development was built around the

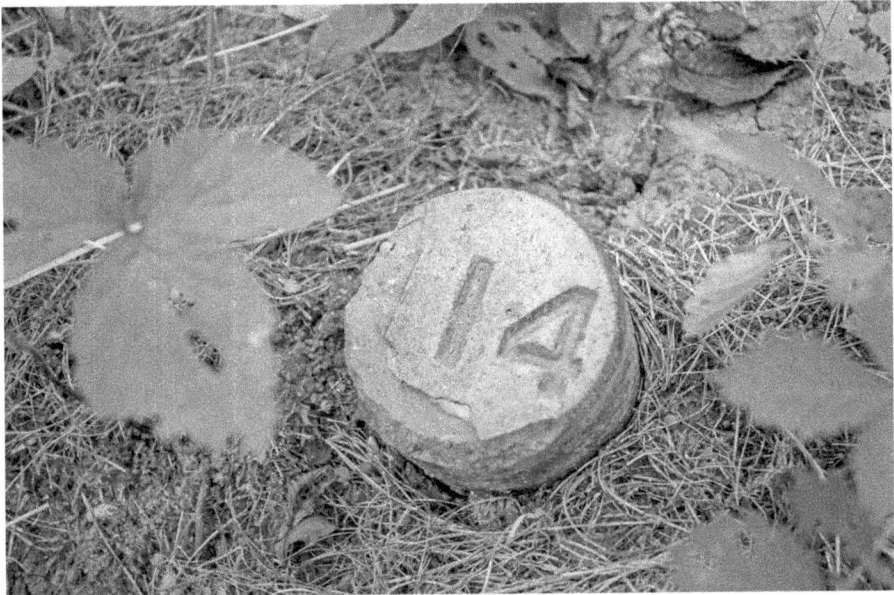

Tile number 114, marking the grave of William Johnson, is still visible today. *Photo by the author.*

The grave of Alexander Baxter (deceased 1908), though obscured by trees and undergrowth, remains visible today. *Photo by the author.*

old cemetery. In 1998, a resident of Topaz Circle, located adjacent to the cemetery, called the sheriff after workers began knocking down tile markers during the construction of a sewer line, the *Vindicator* reported in an article titled "Grave Situation, Angry Neighbors React to Bulldozing in Cemetery."

Over the years, the curious have found discarded tile markers in the high weeds near a wooded area where the cemetery once stood. It is not clear how many markers were ultimately destroyed or what became of the corpses, though they most likely are still there. In the woods behind Topaz Circle, a few tile markers can still be found after all these years. Everything from discarded Christmas trees to piles of leaves and grass clippings have been dumped in the area, and there is nothing to mark the cemetery's location. The few tiles left standing are the last testament to the many thousands who came through the doors of the Mahoning Country Infirmary over the years and are the last reminder of the unknown number of inmates buried on infirmary grounds.

4

FROM MONKEY'S NEST TO THE SHARONLINE

A History of the Green Book *in Youngstown*

If you drove down the soot-stained street of North West Avenue in Youngstown in the 1950s, it would not have been surprising to see the likes of B.B. King, Brook Benton or Fats Domino walking out of the modest Black-owned Allison Hotel, located not far from the U.S. Steel Ohio Works. "It was a jewel to me," said Dr. Bennie Allison, who often stayed at the hotel as a young boy. His grandfather, also named Bennie, owned and operated the Allison. "It had a nice restaurant, good cooks. The thing I remember the most is how they housed all those great groups that couldn't go to other hotels. When they would leave, they'd stock up on ham sandwiches and egg sandwiches for the next couple of stops, because they might not find someplace before then where they could eat."

In those days, Black travelers, even those in popular bands, could drive for many miles without finding a restaurant that would serve them. While white performers stayed at places like the Hotel Pick-Ohio downtown, Black artists scrambled to find Black-owned hotels or even private residencies to stay in. That is, until the widespread publication of the *Negro Motorist Green Book*, a travel guide that served African Americans from 1936 to 1967.

When Jim Crow ruled the South and de facto segregation existed in much of the rest of the country, the *Green Book* guide served as a lifeline for Black travelers who had few options for food, shelter or even gasoline during extended trips away from home. Author Candacy Taylor has referred to it as the "Overground Railroad." In the 1940s, journalist George Schuyler estimated that Black travelers could stay at perhaps 6 percent of the country's "better hotels and motels." He estimated that by 1949, there were "probably fewer than twenty cities in the country where Negroes are not completely barred from white-owned restaurants."

In this environment, several travel guides existed for African Americans at one time or another, including *Go, Guide to Pleasant Motoring*; *Travel Guide of Negro Hotels and Guest Houses*; and *Bronze American National Travel Guide*. The *Green Book* was the longest lasting of them. Many Esso gas stations, which routinely provided service to African Americans, distributed the guides. The *Green Book* eventually listed 9,500 establishments. Numbers are not exactly known, but at one point it is thought that about fifteen thousand copies a year were produced. Initially, the guide, a product of the mind of postal carrier Victor Hugo Green, listed only locations in the New York City area. As time passed, it encompassed most of America, Canada and overseas locations. The pages of the *Green Book* did include Black-friendly white establishments, Taylor writes, but it also served as a compendium of Black-owned businesses, which ultimately helped both Black business owners and travelers.

According to the *Youngstown Vindicator*, in 1950, the Youngstown area produced "more steel per square mile or per capita than any similar spot on earth." Plentiful jobs in the local mills attracted large numbers of African Americans moving northward as part of the Great Migration, one of the largest internal migrations in American history—and with them came new Black-owned businesses. At its peak in 1950, Youngstown (population 168,000) had twenty-four businesses listed in the *Green Book*. Warren had one business, Lynum and Germans' Cocktail Bar, listed in 1940 on Pine Avenue.

Bennie Allison was part of that migration. He and his wife built the Allison Hotel in 1952 in an area near the Mahoning River called Monkey's Nest. "He built the hotel himself. He laid the bricks and everything," Dr. Allison said. According to local lore, the area's nickname emerged after a band of monkeys escaped from a touring circus in the early 1900s, fanning out through the neighborhood. However, the name proved controversial as more African Americans began to locate there in the 1930s. By the 1950s, most of the residents were Black, and a Black business district served the community in the nearby Westlake Crossing area. The Allison proved to be in a perfect location.

Dr. Allison regularly met performers, like a young Stevie Wonder, during his weekends at the hotel. "On the nights they [bands] played, the hotel substituted as a dancehall after the shows were over," he said. The hotel contained only about twenty rooms. "It was just about big enough to hold all the band members." Many of the bands staying at the hotel played at the Nu

Elms Ballroom on Youngstown's north side, one of the few large dance halls that regularly admitted Black patrons, albeit on select nights. Allison also offered services to other Black travelers. "For the younger men who came by themselves, my father had a house on Burnett Street," Dr. Allison said. "It was like a speakeasy. They had about six or seven bedrooms in that place. They played Pokeno, and they danced."

Urban planners eventually targeted Monkey's Nest for destruction, threatening the hotel's future. The neighborhood was ultimately cleared through eminent domain in the early 1960s to make way for a light industrial area and Interstate Route 680, which today runs through the heart of the old neighborhood, now known as the Riverbend. The nearby U.S. Route 422 project, the building of I-680 and the urban renewal–inspired clearing of Monkey's Nest caused many Black businesses to suffer, relocate or disappear entirely. This proved emblematic of urban renewal in the country at large. "In most traditional African American neighborhoods, *Green Book* buildings were destroyed in the name of urban renewal," Candacy Taylor writes. After relocating to the north side, the Allison Hotel survived until the late 1980s, well after the era of the *Green Book*. However, younger generations failed to support the motel, Dr. Allison said, and it ultimately closed.

Like the Allison Hotel, most *Green Book* sites are long gone. Only about a third of all sites once listed in the guide are still standing, according to the documentary *The Green Book: Guide to Freedom*. All the Youngstown music establishments listed in the *Green Book* have been demolished. Drummer Shedrick Hobbs, who once played with the likes of Charlie Parker and Melvin Wanzo, recalled the clubs that Blacks could patronize during the *Green Book* era. "There used to be the Silver Dollar, the Sportere, 40 Club and the Shrine Club. On the west side was the West Side Social [Club], and a little further down was the Black and Tan."

The West Side Social Club, Sportere and 40 Club were listed in the *Green Book*. The Black and Tan, named for a term once used to describe integrated clubs where Black and white mixed, stood at the site of the former Cotton Club in Monkey's Nest. A Black businessman named William "Uncle Billy" Rideout once operated the establishment when it was located on East Federal Street. He also operated the Rideout Hotel, which was listed in the *Green Book*. Artists such as Bill Doggett, Lynn Hope and Count Basie played many of these venues. However, most Mahoning Valley clubs were open to Black performers but not Black audiences, Hobbs said. "Back then, the only way a black guy got into a lot of these clubs was if you were playing. You weren't allowed to go sit up there and listen. You could work there, but that was it."

Black travelers coming to Youngstown in 1950 could find more than music and a place to stay. One could eat at the Bagnet Restaurant on the far west end of downtown or head down the street for a haircut at Harris's barbershop. For a drink, the State Tavern in the downtown beckoned. You could even get your suit jacket adjusted at Henry Walker Tailors. If you needed gas or your car serviced, Hall's garage could help you. Yet once again, urban renewal conspired against many of these *Green Book* businesses. The city nearly tore down the east end of downtown in the late 1960s and early 1970s. The victims included clubs, bars, hotels, barbershops and tailors. Today, there's hardly any evidence these establishments ever existed.

Far across town on the east side, many years after the 1960s, Theresa Lyons moved to a new home. In the basement she found a cast-iron press for pressing sheets, and in one of the floorboards she found a postcard for the Sepia Red Lion Motel, which the home's former occupants, Grace and Price Lyons, once operated just next door. "If you walk through the backyard, you can see there are parts of the old blacktop all through the area," Lyons (no relation) said. Still visible among the underbrush are the outlines of the long-since-demolished buildings Grace and Price advertised as "the first colored motel" in Mahoning Valley.

Price Lyons was born in Pittsburgh in 1915. An amateur boxer turned entrepreneur, he moved to Youngstown in 1944 and opened the Red Lion in 1949. The hotel handled its share of families and lone travelers, but popular musical acts also found their way to the Red Lion via the *Green Book*, said Dr. Allison. "The Red Lion dealt with a lot of stars," he said. Many of them—including Duke Ellington, Peg Leg Bates and Jackie Wilson—stayed at the hotel on the east side of Youngstown while on their way to play at the

A postcard image depicts the Sepia Red Lion Motel on Coitsville-Hubbard Road. *Courtesy of Theresa Lyons.*

The former Grace Lyons Sepia Restaurant, now a VFW post, is one of two sites connected to the *Green Book* still standing. *Photo by the author.*

Twin City Elks, a popular music venue located across the state line in Farrell, Pennsylvania. According to Dr. Allison, the Red Lion was the last safe stop before coming to the city of Hubbard, just outside of Youngstown, which was known for not welcoming Black travelers.

In 1963, the Lyonses expanded their operation and opened the Grace Lyons Sepia Restaurant near the motel. Available for breakfast, lunch and dinner, the restaurant featured a cocktail lounge and a private banquet room capable of holding 120 guests. "A lot of clients of the motel went to that place," Theresa Lyons said. The opening advertisement for the restaurant in the *Vindicator* featured a Black family, something exceedingly rare for the time.

While the Red Lion Motel has since been demolished, the former restaurant is now home to a Veteran of Foreign Wars post. The building is one of only two sites connected to the *Green Book* still standing in Youngstown.

Until recently, there were three. The city demolished the abandoned Wee Motel on the east side in August 2019, erasing the last of the eight Youngstown motels once listed in the *Green Book*. Barbara Stevens lived at the Wee with her mother and sister in the late 1950s. "We had our own little apartment separate from the motel," she remembered. Her mother helped run the establishment, and Stevens spent many days helping her. "I had to mangle sheets and pillowcases after they came out of the dryer," she recalled.

Stevens's grandfather Carl B. Howard Sr. built the motel with the help of her father. They named it the M&H Motel. After her grandfather died, her uncle Wallace Mitchell bought the motel. The new name he chose for the motel, Wee, stood for Wallace, Emmiline (his wife) and Edith (Stevens's mother). "My mother worked very hard at that place to help make it as nice as it was," Stevens said. Mitchell and Emmiline were both prominent members of the Black community. He was an exalted ruler of the local Buckeye Elks and served as the commander of the George Washington Carver Post 504 of the American Legion. "She [Emmiline] was a very prominent hairdresser in those days," Stevens said. "She had her own beauty shop connected to a house on the south side of Youngstown."

Farther down the road from the Wee was the Sharonline, which became a notable Black neighborhood in the city. "A lot of prominent Black people moved out there at that time because the land was abundant," Stevens said. In time, McGuffey Road, where the Wee was located, became an important commercial corridor on the east side, bringing more traffic to the motel. In 1962, a photo of the Wee appeared in the *Green Book*. The

The long-abandoned Wee Motel stood on McGuffey Road until 2019. *Photo by the author.*

accompanying advertisement listed sixteen units and a coffee shop. Unlike many establishments listed in the *Green Book*, the motel survived the decades after the 1964 Civil Rights Act. Wallace died in 1987, and the Wee closed soon after. In 2018, the release of the Academy Award–winning movie *Green Book* brought renewed attention to the abandoned motel. However, time and the elements had taken a toll on the old building, which the city soon demolished.

The last of the local *Green Book* sites still standing is perhaps the most important and one that should not be forgotten. What became known as the West Federal Street YMCA, or the "Colored Y," emerged from the racial politics that developed during the first wave of the Great Migration. As World War I unfolded in 1914, American manufacturers found themselves cut off from their traditional supply of immigrant labor in Europe. The steel mills in Youngstown began to draw from a new labor supply, the thousands and eventually millions of African Americans fleeing the harsh world of sharecropping in the Jim Crow South. In the 1920s, Youngstown's Black community more than doubled, from about 6,600 to nearly 15,000.

At the same time, the Ku Klux Klan emerged as a major political force in the Mahoning Valley. In 1923, Klan-backed candidate Charles Scheible won the mayoral race in Youngstown. Approximately fifty thousand Klan members from three states gathered in the Youngstown area to celebrate the Klan's victories in the mayoral, city council and school board elections. Historian William Jenkins states that the local Klan's members mostly joined to "preserve 'American' cultural dominance" over recent immigrants. However, Youngstown's small but growing Black population was not unaffected. According to noted Youngstown educator Dr. Herbert Armstrong, the activities of the Klan helped drive away the customer base of his grandfather Fletcher Armstrong's haberdashery, which was the first Black-owned business of its kind in Youngstown. An October 22, 1923 interview with a local Klan representative revealed the organization's desire to see segregated seating on the city's streetcar line. The *Vindicator* ran the interview under the title "Klan Wants Jim Crow Cars, Opposes Catholic Schools." The Klan's popularity, undone by corruption and national scandal, did not survive the 1920s, and the organization faded away by the time of the Depression.

During the 1930s, according to historian George D. Beelen, recent African American migrants from the South protested the refusal of many West Federal Street eateries to serve Black patrons—including all the Isaly's stores in the Youngstown area. Nevertheless, segregation persisted in everything from the local retail trade to the city's public pools (and the large privately owned pool at Idora Park). In this environment, a movement rooted in Black nationalism and Black self-sufficiency began to take root in the 1920s. Marcus Garvey's Universal Negro Improvement Association (UNIA) gained notable support among Ohio cities, according to historian Mark Christian. The UNIA opened "Liberty Halls" around the area, including West Federal Street just outside downtown. Garvey even spoke in Youngstown in 1923. UNIA activities and other programs centered on Black community improvement ultimately found a home at the Booker T. Washington Settlement on West Federal Street. The settlement house was in many ways the forerunner to the West Federal Street YMCA. It provided a much-needed venue for recreation and social services for the Black community.

In the late 1920s, the YMCA board of trustees ruled that the central Y would not be open to activities "of a social or physical nature where we are not yet able to get our white friends to permit an intermingling." To counter this act of segregation, the local Black community sought its own branch of the Y. It started with just two rooms at the Lee Tire building on the east side, but in 1931, the $200,000 West Federal Street YMCA facility opened on the site of the old Booker T. Washington Settlement.

Dr. Simeon Booker Sr., the institution's first director, and John Chase helped shepherd the Y into existence. Booker assisted in the opening of a similar facility for the Black community in Baltimore and helped obtain a $25,000 Julius Rosenwald grant for part of the Youngstown Y's construction. Chase, future superintendent of the Youngstown Playground Association, initially corresponded with W.E.B. Du Bois about a strategy for boycotting the YMCA before settling on the idea of opening a separate branch. The new Y debuted in 1931. "It was the finest African American Y in the country at the time," said local Y historian Al Leonhart. According to historian Nina Mjagkij, it was one of eleven YMCA buildings erected across the country for African Americans between 1924 and 1933. A separate YWCA had existed for Black women and girls since 1919. The facilities occupied a large house on Belmont Avenue. "Ours is almost, if not the only, meeting place for Negro women of Youngstown," Executive Secretary Alice Warner Parham told the *Vindicator* in 1940.

Green Book travelers could enjoy the facilities at both the YMCA and the YWCA. The YMCA cafeteria was listed in the guide as a restaurant. For motorists looking for a safe place to stay, a shower and a hot meal, it proved an ideal spot. For the Black community in Youngstown, it represented

The women of the Belmont YWCA pose in an undated photograph. *Courtesy of the author.*

much more. The Y taught their children how to swim, provided an outlet for cultural and educational activities and introduced young men and women to mentors in the community. "You would plan programs for clubs, and speakers came in," James Lottier, the physical director, later told the Youngstown State University Oral History Program. "They tried to teach you in a manner to give you some incentive to try and make something out of your life." Generations of Black Youngstowners passed through the Y's doors before it was ultimately closed in 1974, years after the last edition of the *Green Book*. Yet many in the Black community fought to save the West Federal Street location, but not out of a desire to maintain segregation. "In 1955, the board finally voted to allow African Americans at the central branch," Leonhart said. "And there was a very, very small trickle. Most everyone stayed at West Federal."

"Many of us felt that the central YMCA could not do the job that the West Federal Street branch had done and could continue to do," attorney Floyd Haynes later told the *Vindicator.* For years, the Rescue Mission of the Mahoning Valley occupied the old Y. However, after the organization broke ground at a new location, the fate of the former West Federal Street branch building is now uncertain. No marker identifies the building as a historical *Green Book* site, and it is possible that it may have a future date with the wrecking ball.

The West Federal Street YMCA, or "Colored Y," as it was sometimes called, served the Black community from 1931 until 1974. *Courtesy of the author.*

Members of St. Augustine's Episcopal Church basketball team pose for a portrait at the West Federal Street YMCA. *Courtesy of Stacey Adger.*

Many historians and historical preservationists now call for the preservation of structures once listed in the *Green Book*. In the documentary *The Green Book: Guide to Freedom*, Dr. Henrie Monteith Treadwell summed up what she considers to be the importance of the travel guide: "It's important to have everyone in this nation examine the significance of the *Green Book*," she said. "If you don't see the history, if you don't see where it was, how can you say it happened? We need to find those places, and we need to see them, and we need to revere what they meant, because they made all of the difference to our survival."

5

THE WPA IN THE MAHONING VALLEY

*Give a man a dole and you save his body and destroy his spirit. Give him a job
and pay him an assured wage, and you save both body and spirit.*
—Harry Hopkins

In 1930, Youngstown reached its peak population of 170,000, making it the forty-fifth-largest city in the country. Warren, the second-largest city in Mahoning Valley, boasted a 51 percent increase in population since 1920, bringing its population to over 41,000. In 1927, the Youngstown steel district had been the biggest producer of steel in the country. Youngstown's laborers earned the highest average wages of any manufacturing workers in comparable industrial cities.

Yet these numbers belied the dark times that the Mahoning Valley had entered as the Great Depression tightened its grip on America during the early 1930s. In the spring of 1932, Youngstown mayor Joseph Heffernan wrote an article for the *Atlantic* titled "The Hungry City: A Mayor's Experience with Unemployment." In graphic detail, the mayor described a visit he made to an abandoned police station the city had converted into a shelter for the ever-increasing numbers of homeless:

*I heartily wish that those folks who have made themselves comfortable by
ignoring and denying the suffering of their less fortunate neighbors could
see some of the sights I saw. There were old men gnarled by heavy labor,
young mechanics tasting the first bitterness of defeat, clerks and white-*

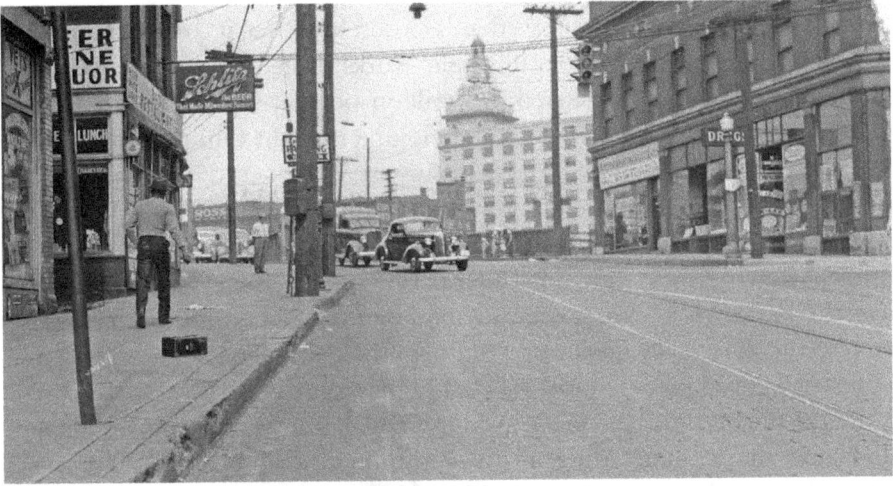

The Spring Common area of Youngstown as it appeared during the Depression. *Courtesy of Thomas Molocea.*

collar workers learning the equality of misery, derelicts who fared no worse in bad times than in good, Negroes who only a short time before had come from southern cotton fields, now glad to find any shelter from the cold, immigrants who had been lured to [the] "land of youth and freedom"— each one a personal tragedy and all together an overwhelming catastrophe for the Nation.

As the official unemployment rate exceeded 25 percent in late 1932, Democratic candidate Franklin Delano Roosevelt defeated incumbent Herbert Hoover—who had been widely blamed for failing to act in the face of the economic catastrophe—and was inaugurated in March 1933. Over the next two years, a variety of "alphabet soup" agencies emerged to deal with the growing economic and unemployment crisis. Lumped together, these programs came to be described as Roosevelt's "New Deal" for America. It proved to be a unique moment. "The New Deal made as clear a break with policy tradition as any in American history," writes historian Jefferson Cowie.

Few New Deal programs exemplified that break with tradition more than the Works Progress Administration. The agency came out of the Emergency Relief Appropriation Act of 1935, which represented the largest public-assistance work programs in the nation's history. The WPA was directed at what Roosevelt called the "forgotten man." Headed by

Harry Hopkins, one of the president's closest advisors, it sought to employ out-of-work men and women in public-works projects across the country. During its height, it employed 3.3 million people, making it the largest employer in the country. Approximately one in eight Ohioans worked for the WPA between 1935 and 1941. In August 1935, nearly 1,000 men were pulled out of unemployment and into the ranks of the WPA in Mahoning. Ralph Vail, the local WPA administrator, had wandered the countryside until he found work with the Federal Emergency Relief Administration and the WPA. "Like many others, I had plenty of good jobs in my time," he told the *Youngstown Vindicator*, "but with the depression, the construction industry went to pieces, and I was left high and dry."

By the fall of 1935, the WPA in Mahoning County employed 4,000 men, and after the women's program was instituted, a total of 7,400 workers labored on local projects. By early 1936, WPA workers had improved ninety miles of Mahoning County roads and completely built another forty-two. The *Vindicator* reported that, according to a local woman, "Doctors will be accessible now, their children can go to school without being carried miles in the mud, snow and ice to a school bus."

Over 17.0 miles of road in the Youngstown metropolitan area—including Bears Dens, Midlothian Boulevard and Shady Run Road—had already been built by early 1936, with curbing and ditches constructed. WPA workers improved roads and built 8.8 miles of footpaths in Mill Creek Park. In total, they eventually created 1,500 feet of trails in the park and constructed numerous dry-stone wall embankments. According to historian John C. Melnick, they built another nine holes at the Mill Creek Park golf course, restored parts of the old mill and installed a sewage disposal system. They crafted the Bruce Rogers stone bridge and the stone bridge between the upper and lower meadows in Bears Den. WPA workers were responsible for building large stone retaining walls along the west side of Lake Cohasset and along the Artist's Trail. Unemployed musicians even found work teaching music classes at the park. "The beautiful artistic creations by the WPA in Mill Creek Park are of sturdy structure, lasting beauty and a challenge to present day workers and contractors," Melnick stated in the 1970s.

In his autobiography, famed attorney, judge and civil rights activist Nathaniel R. Jones recalls the impact the WPA had on his old neighborhood of Smoky Hollow. Jones lived in the middle of an unpaved street that frequently fell victim to gravel and mudslides during storms. The WPA gave much-needed employment to the largely immigrant population of the Hollow, who helped finally pave his street. "The WPA went a long way

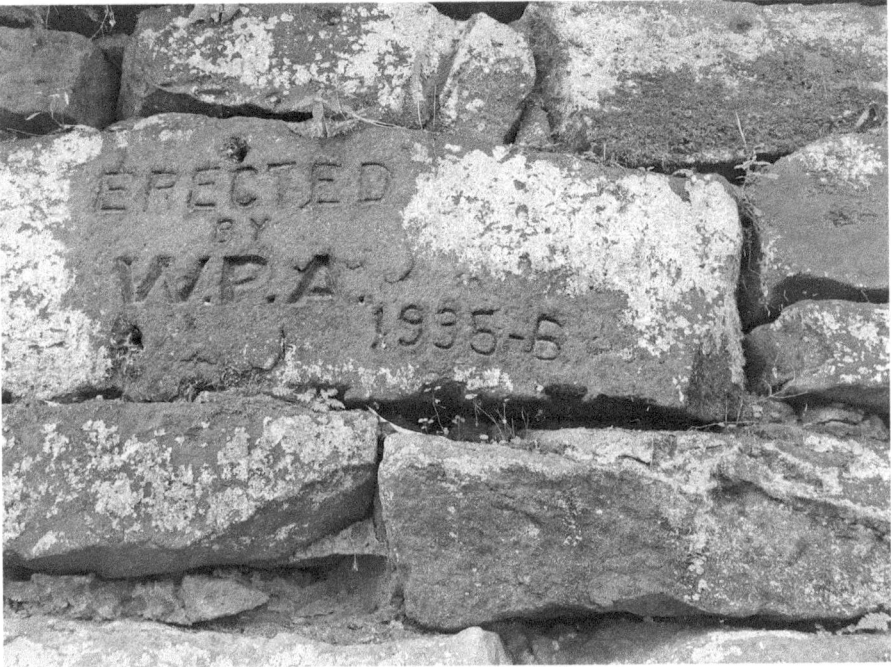

Above: A WPA inscription remains visible on a retaining wall on the "Artist's Trail" in Mill Creek Park. *Photo by the author.*

Left: Lowellville City Hall, one of several city halls built or improved by the WPA. *Photo by the author.*

The WPA Memorial Building opened as a community building in Canfield in 1937. *Courtesy of the author.*

toward relieving the pain caused by the Depression," he writes. "Many of the WPA workers who transformed the street were neighbors and members of our church."

WPA projects in Mahoning encompassed both the large and the small. Workers helped build city hall in Lowellville and Milton Township, a viaduct on South Schenley Avenue, a pavilion at Crandall Park, a 3,800-seat grandstand at the county fairgrounds, a high school stadium in Struthers and fire stations in Austintown and Boardman. They sealed fifty abandoned mines and did extensive work at the Canfield Experimental Farm. WPA labor rewired, repaired, painted and installed retaining walls at schools all over the valley. They also built sewage disposal plants for the Mahoning County Infirmary and the city of Sebring. A grant of more than $109,000 went toward the creation of Roosevelt Park in Campbell. In Canfield, $65,000 in federal funds and WPA labor constructed the WPA Memorial Building, which housed a branch of the Reuben McMillan Free Library and the Roxy Theater. Appropriately enough, a picture of President Roosevelt was placed inside the building's cornerstone. In early 1939, the WPA reviewed and sent to the Civil Aeronautics Authority a proposal for what would be the largest WPA project in Mahoning Valley. Approximately one thousand men labored on the construction of the six-hundred-acre Youngstown Municipal Airport, which opened in Vienna Township in 1940.

Non-infrastructure-related projects also engaged workers throughout the area. The WPA began a grave registration survey that employed 1,300 workers across Ohio and sought to identify the graves of every unknown solider buried in the state. They held vocational classes in Youngstown to train workers for manual occupations in local industries. The WPA sent men and women from Niles to Kent State University for recreational training so they could properly supervise the playgrounds being built in Trumbull County.

Warren resident Gertrude Hendricks worked on one of these types of projects as a home economics supervisor of women's projects for the WPA from 1935 to 1939. "The depression was deep. People didn't have jobs, but there was some WPA work," she later told the YSU Oral History Program. Her work covered five counties: Trumbull, Ashtabula, Portage, Mahoning and Columbiana. "We worked on sewing projects; we had housekeeping aid projects; we had school lunch projects," Hendricks explained.

The building of the Youngstown Municipal Airport in Vienna served as a kind of capstone project for the WPA in the Mahoning Valley. *Courtesy of Thomas Molocea.*

We did home work, that is housework for people who were physically unable to do it. At that time, we just had workers who needed employment, and they worked for a living wage, and they were sent into homes to work. This was for the housekeeping aids. As supervisor of women's professional projects, I had all the records projects too, where we were copying records that were in the courthouses. Then they would put the original records in a vault and preserve those and leave the copies for the attorneys to use.

In the fall of 1939, First Lady Eleanor Roosevelt visited Youngstown and reported on some of the WPA projects she saw for her syndicated newspaper column:

I saw two WPA projects during the morning. One, a visual education project in a school, was turning out extremely good material such as posters, pictures of birds, samples of grass, trees, bugs, etc. for use in schools throughout the district. The other, an Ohio State project being carried on in several big cities, I have never happened to come across anywhere else, though it is doubtless being done in many places. Newspapers in the various cities are being indexed and microfilms of the pages are being made. These films can be stored and lent with ease, and the indexing material will make available information on the news for the years which these projects cover. It takes several weeks to train a man for work on this project, which requires intelligence and accuracy.

It is commonly, though incorrectly, believed that murals and artwork featured in several valley post offices were also produced by the WPA. The post office murals were commissioned by the Treasury Section of Painting and Sculpture, which eventually became known as the Section of Fine Arts. Administered by the Procurement Division of the Department of the Treasury, the "Section," as it was often known, recruited artists to produce high-quality works for public facilities throughout the nation. Many of the murals were featured in post offices, as they were often the most publicly accessible building in many communities. Subject matter often featured images of regional industries, landscapes and folkways. Hubert Mesibov's mural, *Steel Industry for Hubbard*, depicts three workers in the crucible of a mill. Glenn M. Shaw's two murals at the Warren post office on High Street also feature men working in the steel industry. The post office in Campbell contains a unique terra-cotta relief depicting men pouring steel. Sadly, a fourth post office mural—titled *Workers of the Soil* and once located

Artist Glenn M. Shaw's murals still grace the inside of the post office on High Street in Warren. The murals were commissioned by the Treasury Section of Painting and Sculpture. *Photo by the author.*

in Girard—has since been destroyed. These local murals form part of a larger national artistic legacy left behind by the section. Undoubtedly, however, few people today are aware of why and when they were made or their historical importance.

For the men toiling on the local WPA projects, their work did not just improve the area; it also proved a vital source of income and self-worth. Don McKenzie excitedly told the *Vindicator* how his job had helped him pay off his home loan. "I am proud to announce that I'm paying back their money. I work for the WPA. I have already paid a little of it back and will pay back every cent." Youngstown resident John Light, formerly employed at the Mahoning Valley Sanitary District, said the WPA provided an opportunity to earn his own paycheck. "I'd rather work anytime for what I get rather than have it handed to me without doing anything for it," he told the *Vindicator* in 1935. "I tried to get along as best I could. I even traveled to Pittsburgh and worked in a steel plant there for several days to get money to keep up. I'm hoping the WPA will continue, and I won't have to worry about getting along."

Administrator Vail praised the work ethic of the men under him in Mahoning County; however, not everyone felt the WPA (or its workers) were of value. John C. Melnick, author of *The Green Cathedral*, relates a story of one motorist in Mill Creek Park who, when told by a flagger that WPA men were up ahead, replied: "That's alright, I wouldn't wake them up!" According to local historian Mark Peyko: "Sometimes local labor unions challenged WPA wage scales and practices. Other times, discontent was internal." In Trumbull County, WPA employees frequently clashed with the county administrator, and 4,800 workers—with the support of the local Workers Alliance of America (WAA), a socialist organization—walked off their projects and went on strike in 1939. The WAA also helped WPA employees in Trumbull County adopt a resolution challenging prevailing wages.

Every municipality that participated in WPA projects had to provide part of the funding to receive federal aid. For example, in 1935, the city of Niles received almost $33,000.00 in federal funds for projects and would be expected to contribute $3,611.00. In 1939, Trumbull County contributed $4.00 toward every WPA employee during a given month. However, officials estimated that it cost the county more than $20.00 a month to support a family on direct relief. In 1936, unskilled workers in Trumbull earned $60.50 a month; semiskilled workers earned anywhere from $65.00 to $70.00; skilled professionals earned from $94.00 to $103.50.

In November 1938, Cuyahoga County had the lowest percentage of its population on direct relief, at 4.79 percent, but at 19 percent, it had the second-highest percentage in the state working for the WPA. By comparison, Mahoning County had 5.13 percent on relief and 12.39 percent working for the WPA. Montgomery County had 5.92 percent on relief and 10.40 percent working for the WPA. Stark County stood at 8.04 percent on relief and 10.90 employed by the WPA. Trumbull County had 5.30 percent on direct relief and 16.25 earning a paycheck from the WPA.

The WPA left a lasting impact on Trumbull County. According to the *Niles Daily Times*, between July 1935 and March 1940, workers built or repaired 109 buildings, which included the construction of Girard City Hall and a new hospital building at the county infirmary. Workers built a gymnasium and an auditorium at Bazetta Township Centralized School. Additions were made to Niles and Brookfield High Schools, and improvements were made to thirty-four other school buildings, the *Daily Times* reported.

They repaired four Warren fire stations, Warren City Hall and the Trumbull County Detention Home. Significant repairs were made to McKinley Memorial in Niles. WPA laborers also modernized the Trumbull County Courthouse, Trumbull Children's Home, Warren City Library and the County Emergency Hospital in Warren. Workers constructed or

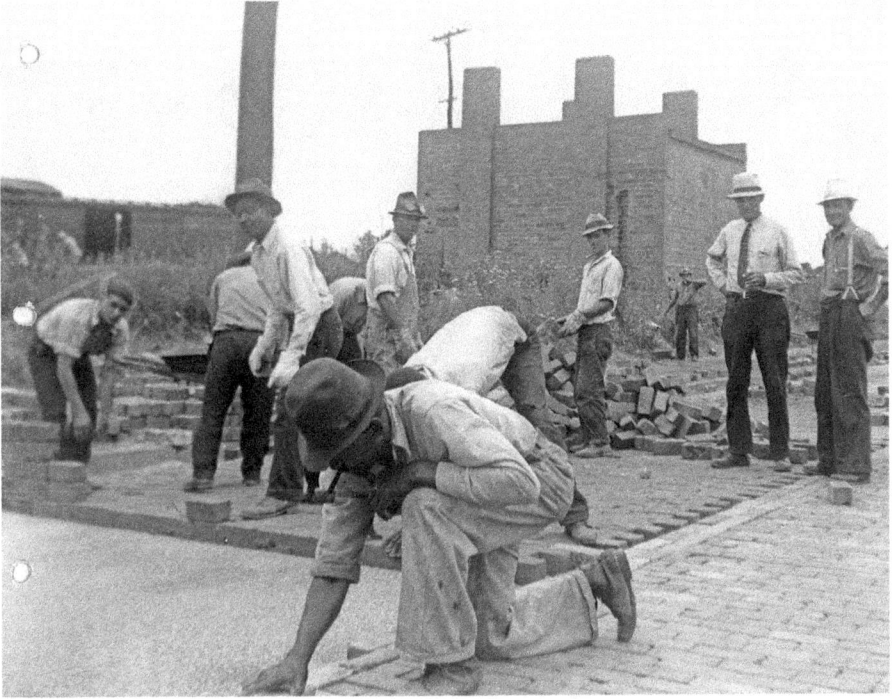

WPA workers relay brick for a project in Trumbull County, circa 1937. *Courtesy of Trumbull Memory Project.*

improved 295 miles of roads and streets and approximately fifty bridges. WPA laborers even installed water lines for rolling mills in Niles. The WPA Education Program held classes in adult literacy in Warren, Niles, Girard and Newton Falls. Unemployed teachers found jobs instructing adults in the basics of reading, spelling and basic arithmetic. In late 1937, the WPA conducted thirty-nine classes across the county with 420 pupils enrolled, according to the *Daily Times*. Approximately 30,000 teachers taught the 2,000,000 adults who enrolled in WPA literacy classes across the country.

All WPA workers were required to register with the state employment service so they could be matched with jobs in private industry—if any were available. Conditions in Youngstown and Mahoning County remained problematic, according to a 1939 report from the United States Conference of Mayors. Youngstown continued to be incapable of fully supporting the number of families on relief. "It is absolutely necessary to maintain present WPA quotas," the report stated. Approximately 7,800 workers continued to be employed by the agency in Mahoning County.

WPA workers construct a sewer system near the corner of Paige Avenue and Dana Street in Warren, circa 1937. *Courtesy of Trumbull Memory Project.*

By 1939, the job market began improving enough to move significant numbers of WPA workers in Trumbull County into new jobs. According to the *Daily Times*, semiskilled and skilled workers increasingly took new jobs in the burgeoning defense industries. Nearly 70 percent of all male WPA workers in Trumbull County in 1941 were over forty-five and categorized as unskilled. Charles Sharp, Akron district WPA manager, told the paper that the average age of a male WPA worker that year was forty-eight. "This is in marked contrast to an estimated average age of 28 years when WPA employment was at its peak in the late fall of 1938," he said.

By the spring of 1941, 1,261 men and 299 women continued to work for the WPA in Trumbull County. In 1943, with the country now embroiled in World War II, the WPA came to an end. The Depression, too, was a thing of the past. "The 25 percent unemployment rate of a decade earlier would reach 1.9 percent in 1943," writes historian Nick Taylor. The next year, it would fall below 1 percent. Breadlines and shantytowns were a bad memory, now that the WPA had made it possible to forget them."

The popularity of New Deal programs such as the WPA helped buoy President Roosevelt's immense popularity in the Mahoning Valley. *Courtesy of Thomas Molocea.*

Be it on the side of a viaduct or the cornerstone of an old building, the mark of the WPA can still be seen by the careful eye today. The generation of workers who passed through the WPA and the Depression is now gone, but their legacy lives on all around us in the built environment of Mahoning Valley.

6

WPA Documented Memories of
Residents Born into Slavery

T
he soot-filled sky of the steel city of Campbell, Ohio, was a world away from where Phoebe Bost started life. In 1936, when she was in her nineties and living with her daughter on the industrial corridor of Wilson Avenue, Bost found herself talking to a perfect stranger in her house. "Their home is fairly well furnished and clean in appearance," the man, Frank Smith, noted at the time. "Phoebe is of slender stature and is quite active in spite of the fact that she is nearing her nineties." Smith, one of many out-of-work writers at the time hired by the federal government, had come from the WPA (Works Progress Administration) Federal Writers' Project to interview Bost. Many decades earlier, and a thousand miles from Campbell, she had started life enslaved in the world of the antebellum South.

Bost was uncertain of her real age. She had been sold at a slave auction in Baltimore by her first master to a man named Vaul Mooney. An apparently harsh master, Mooney forbade any singing or dancing on his plantation and never failed to administer "a whipping at the slightest provocation," Smith wrote. Bost acted as a nursemaid for her master's children. "I had to hol' the baby all de time she slept," she said, "and sometimes I got so sleepy myself that I had to prop ma' eyes open with pieces of whisks from a broom."

This painful conversation was recorded as part of what the Library of Congress calls "one of the most enduring and noteworthy achievements of the WPA." The WPA was multifaceted. At its height, it employed millions of unemployed men and women to work at everything from paving roads

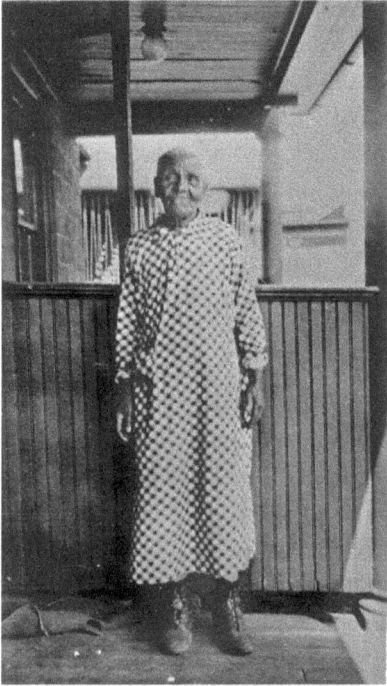

Campbell resident Phoebe Bost began her life enslaved on a plantation in Louisiana. *Courtesy of Library of Congress, Federal Writers' Project, United States Work Progress Administration.*

to recording symphonies. In 1936, the Federal Writers' Project (FWP) sent out writers to accomplish a unique task: document the stories of the last of the country's formerly enslaved men and women. According to historian Catherine Stewart, author of *Long Past Slavery: Representing Race in the Federal Writers' Project*, the FWP "intended to record the history of slavery as well as African American folk culture from those who had experienced it firsthand."

Interviewers were trained on which questions to ask and how to capture the dialects of those they interviewed, something that can offend contemporary audiences, the Library of Congress emphasizes. They ultimately interviewed 2,300 African Americans across the country, including 32 in Ohio (27 interviews did not make it to the Library of Congress and are available through the Ohio Historical Society) and 3 in the Mahoning Valley, as part of what eventually became the seventeen volumes of edited transcripts called *Slave Narratives: A Folk History of Slavery in the United States from Interviews with Former Slaves.*

At the end of the Civil War, over 90 percent of Blacks lived in the South. By the time Bost was interviewed, millions of African Americans had left during the first wave of what historians refer to as the "Great Migration." America's entry into World War I brought with it a demand for labor in industrial cities like Youngstown. In addition, the indignities of Jim Crow and a devastating boll weevil epidemic in the cotton-growing regions of the South helped produce a flood of African Americans coming north. The migration had begun. By the time Frank Smith interviewed Melissa (Lowe) Barden in 1936, over 14,500 African Americans called Youngstown home. Barden lived with her daughter in the Sharonline, a neighborhood where many of the southern migrants to the city settled. "I's way up yonder somewheres maybe 80 or 90 years," she told Smith.

Barden lost her sight to cataracts, but she could still recall her years in bondage. Born on a plantation in Chattooga County, Georgia, she said her master, whose name she later took, was a kindly man. She recalled singing folk songs such as "Sho' Fly Go 'Way from Me" and dancing. However, a darkness belied her tale. Her master had sold her mother and gave away one of her sisters as a wedding present to his daughter, who later sold her. Following emancipation, Barden's mother sought out her four lost daughters but was able to find only Melissa. Mother and daughter went to work for wages on another plantation in Newton County, Georgia. After her mother died, Melissa married a man named Barden.

FWP interviewers took portraits of five hundred of the individuals they interviewed. When Smith asked Barden if he could take her photo, she replied, "All right, but don't you-all poke fun at me because I am just as God made me." With hands folded in her lap, Barden, though blind, seems to look out far beyond her porch. She is long since passed, but her old home still stands on Jacobs Road. It is the only residence of the three women interviewed in Mahoning Valley still standing today.

The home of Angeline Lester has long since been torn down. Frank Smith described it as "a very dilapidated one-story structure, which once was a retail storeroom with an addition built on the rear at a different floor level." When Smith interviewed Lester, she lived alone with several chickens and cats on a stretch of West Federal Street near several predominately Black neighborhoods. The city later bulldozed most of the area during urban renewal. Lester began her life on a plantation in Stewart County, Georgia, around 1847. When she was four, her father was sold to a plantation near Brooksville, Georgia. Her mother and sister were sold to a plantation in Randolph County, Georgia. Liberation for her eventually came when Union soldiers entered the county in 1865. "Angeline remembers the [Confederate] soldiers coming to the plantation, but any news about the war was kept from them," Smith wrote.

After news of the defeat of the Confederacy spread, Lester recalled a celebration among the freed slaves in Benevolence, Georgia. She told Smith it was the first time she had ever tasted roasted meat. A week later, her master informed all of those on the plantation that they were now free. He offered to accommodate anyone who wanted to stay and work for wages, but anyone wishing to leave could take with them only the clothes on their back. "We couldn't tote away much clothes, because we were only given one pair of shoes and two dresses a year," Lester said.

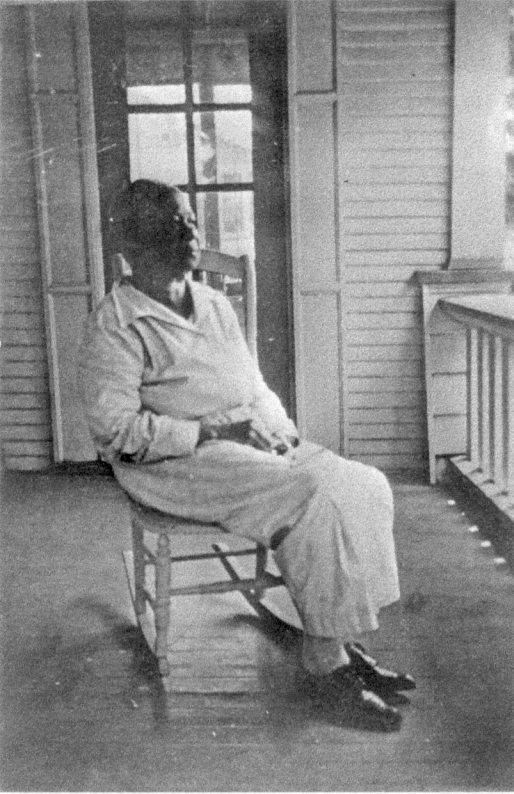

Left: Melissa (Lowe) Barden poses for a portrait during her 1936 interview with WPA writer Frank Smith. *Courtesy of Library of Congress, Federal Writers' Project, United States Work Progress Administration.*

Below: Melissa Barden's house still stands eighty-four years after her interview with the WPA. *Photo by the author.*

She chose to leave after her long-lost father returned to find her. "My father came and gathered us up and took us away, and we worked for different white folks for money." After the death of her father and mother, she married a man named Lester.

Angeline Lester lived in several places in the North. "Worked for De Laud in New Castle, Pennsylvania, and I's worked for De Laud in Akron," she said. Lester's religious faith kept her going, and she felt an obligation to God to remain strong, she explained. "De Laud does not want me to smoke, or drink even tea or coffee. I must keep my strength to work for De Laud." After Smith took her portrait, she asked what would become of it. He told her it would go to Columbus or Washington, D.C. "Lawsy me, if you had tol' me befo' I'd fixed up a bit," she replied.

Angeline Lester survived slavery in the South before finding her way to West Federal Street in Youngstown. *Courtesy of Library of Congress, Federal Writers' Project, United States Work Progress Administration.*

Their exact number is unknown, but freedmen and women had a longer and deeper history in the area than the WPA writers likely realized. Jacob Dent, born in slavery in Petersburg, Virginia, in 1855, did not make into the slave narrative project. He made his way to Youngstown after emancipation and lived in the city for seventy years, retiring from Republic Iron and Steel. He died in 1953 at age ninety-eight. Abe Mason, born enslaved in 1839, died in Youngstown two years before the slave narrative project began at age ninety-five. He had come to the city in 1926. The formerly enslaved Margaret Battery, ninety-nine, was reportedly the oldest woman in the city of Girard when she died in 1935—only a year before the WPA writers began their work.

Longevity appeared to be at least somewhat commonplace among the ex-slaves of the Mahoning Valley. Phoebe Bost, one of the three interviewed by WPA writers, died in 1946 at the reported age of 103. She is interred at Tod Cemetery. Maria Wanser, who in some obituaries is said to have claimed that she served President Lincoln in the White House, was also long-lived. Her exact date of birth is unknown, but a family letter later reprinted in the *Vindicator* suggested she was 103 when she died in 1904. Wanser grew up on a plantation in Fredericksburg, Virginia. It's likely that Wanser was one of the ten thousand enslaved people in that area who crossed over to Union lines in 1862 after the Union army occupied nearby Stafford. She settled in Youngstown in 1868. "Her memory was no less remarkable than her physical vitality," her obituary reads, "and she recalled and described scenes and incidences of the war and of the years preceding it as vividly as if they had happened yesterday."

Researchers today are still attempting to document the lives and stories of the freedmen and women who settled in Mahoning Valley. "It is important to preserve, understand and appreciate the histories and experiences of all people who participated in the creation of this country," said local genealogist Stacey Adger. "By not honoring the stories of all, you cannot tell the complete story of who we are as a nation."

7

The Night East Youngstown Burned

A History of the 1915–1916 Steel Strike

T he Steel Valley has witnessed more than its share of strikes over
the years. From the 1959 steel strike, the largest in the history of
the industry, to the violent clashes of the 1937 "Little Steel" strike,
standoffs between labor and industry are recalled by many current and
former residents. One of the most violent and perhaps most consequential
strikes in both local and national history, however, is almost forgotten
today in the Mahoning Valley. The 1916 steel strike in the village of East
Youngstown (the modern-day city of Campbell) proved to be "one of the
most dramatic the country has known," according to the *American Labor Year
Book*. It ultimately led to East Youngstown becoming known as Campbell
and resulted in a notable development in the history of modern housing.

America was no stranger to violent strikes and bloody clashes between
labor and management in the early twentieth century: the anthracite coal
strike of 1902, the Colorado labor wars of 1903–4, the Philadelphia general
strike of 1910, the Paint Creek–Cabin Creek strike of 1912, the Copper
Country strike of 1913–14 and many more dominated headlines in the first
fifteen years of the new century. American labor conflicts were proving to
be the most violent in the western world. With war in Europe demanding an
increasingly large amount of steel, the economy and the local steel industry
gained steam heading into 1916. Against this backdrop, workers at the tube
mill of Republic Iron and Steel on Poland Avenue began to walk off the job
on December 27, 1915.

Largely unskilled laborers, hit hard by the rise in prices in 1915, demanded an hourly raise from nineteen and a half cents to twenty-five cents. During this era, most steelworkers labored twelve hours a day, six or seven days a week, in dangerous conditions. On the day a man switched shifts, he worked twenty-four hours straight, something workers referred to as "the long turn." "Gradually grievances piled up," write historians Raymond Boryczka and Lorin Lee Cary in *No Strength without Union*. "When war orders and expanded production created labor shortages and a faster work pace in the city, frustrated workers mobilized spontaneously." Local papers reported that "Wobblie" organizers, as members of the Industrial Workers of the World (IWW) were known, had made their way to the plant. The IWW, a militant industrial union, had been involved in strikes across the country. The American Federation of Labor, which represented skilled workers, also arrived in the area to meet with the electrical workers and other tradesmen.

The first signs of the workers' anger occurred at the Republic plant, according to the *Youngstown Vindicator*. "The strikers made such a demonstration Tuesday morning in their effort to have all of the unskilled and skilled labor come out with them, that the services of several city police were required to reinforce the mill officers." By this time, three hundred to four hundred workers had also gone on strike at the nearby Youngstown Sheet and Tube plant in East Youngstown. On January 6, 1916, the *Vindicator* reported that Republic labor arbitrator James Nutt, who supposedly had never failed to successfully adjudicate a strike, seemed confident the disruption at Republic could be settled in a matter of days. Events, however, soon took a turn for the worst.

On the evening of January 6, around one thousand strikers gathered at the north entrance of Youngstown Sheet and Tube. Several "scab" workers who attempted to enter the plant were assaulted. As the night moved into the early morning, crowds lit bonfires and began singing near the Sheet and Tube hospital on Short Street. By Friday, January 7, Sheet and Tube, Brier Hill Steel and Republic Steel were prepared to offer a wage increase to twenty-two cents an hour to the now sixteen thousand men on strike. The offer had not yet been presented to the workers on Friday before the strike devolved into an armed conflict and subsequent riot in East Youngstown.

In retrospect, it is no surprise that the violence began in the village. At the beginning of the century, the area was mostly rural farmland. After the Youngstown Iron Sheet and Tube Company purchased fallow land in

In the early-morning hours of January 7, crowds lit bonfires, sang and danced near the Sheet and Tube hospital on Short Street. *Courtesy of the National Archives and Records Administration.*

the village, four sheet mills, fourteen double-puddling furnaces, three tube mills and a skelp mill soon emerged on the landscape. The rapidly growing industrial character of the village attracted immigrants from all over central, southern and eastern Europe. By 1916, with a population of ten thousand, East Youngstown was the largest incorporated village in Ohio, according to the *Youngstown Telegram*, yet it lacked almost every conceivable facet of modern living.

Today, the city of Campbell is often known as "the city of churches" At the time, however, it was more noted for its drinking establishments. East Youngstown boasted eighteen saloons, yet the village had little in the way of modern infrastructure. Writing for *Survey*, a magazine that focused on political and social issues, John A. Fitch described the unsanitary conditions that predominated in and around the hovels of the village in 1916: "I talked with a man who lived with his wife and three other children in two rooms, for which he paid $7 a month. The other three rooms of the house were occupied by a family of six who paid $9 a month. The house had running water but no bathroom or toilet." Streets were not paved, and outdoor privies were the norm, Smith noted:

As East Youngstown is a village of more recent origin, one need not to be surprised, perhaps, at the lack of sewers and running water....But the mud of the unpaved streets of that desolated [sic] village—mud nearly hub deep, a clinging, all-pervasive mud that plasters itself on shoes and trouser-legs, distributes itself over sidewalks, up from steps and across thresholds, a tell-tale record of a town's perambulations—seems somehow to be symbolic of the community's civic development and its regards for human values.

The violence itself began on Friday afternoon, when Sheet and Tube guards standing on a footbridge above Wilson Avenue confronted strikers. Many years later, eyewitness John Ross described the scene for the Youngstown State University Oral History Program. "Under the bridge there must have been 250 or 200 men. Sheet and Tube had to ask for some protection, so they got the sheriff...deputized maybe twenty-five, thirty, or forty Sheet and Tube workers, people that they trusted."

There is debate over what exactly happened next. Ross claimed the company guards fired on the strikers below after some members of the crowd began throwing stones. Wounded men were quickly dragged away from the scene. Several men who were shot but not too badly injured took refuge in a nearby drugstore. "In a few minutes after the first shot rang out," the *Vindicator* reported, "flames shot from the frame office at the East Youngstown side of the Sheet and Tube bridge."

As more buildings went up in flames, rioters prevented firefighters from putting out the blaze, according to the *Vindicator*. Nearly twelve hours of looting and chaos ensued. The sheriff, heretofore paralyzed by indecision, formed a posse and confronted looters on Washington Street. A shootout ensued, and the suspects fled under the cover of darkness. "Many narrow escapes were experienced when brick walls of buildings fell into the street," the *Vindicator* reported, "carrying wires and telephone poles with them." Local historian Florence Galida later described the scene as told to her by Mary Hoffman Tomich, a child at the time who was at a moving-picture show as the riot broke out: "Many of the children were attending the movie houses on Robinson Road because they had been let out of school early.... Mrs. Tomich was in the movie theater at the time, and the men came in to stop the movie and get the children out. The children were fascinated by the flames. They watched the people looting stores, saw men carrying mattresses up the street and passing cases of pop around. The men passed out lace handkerchiefs to the children."

The Vacca building, erected in 1913, was one of many structures burned during the January 1916 maelstrom. *Courtesy of Thomas Molocea.*

Businesses and dwellings alike vanished in the inferno as night turned into early morning. The conflict did not spread outside of East Youngstown, but nearby Struthers lost power, and people there lined the streets, watching the fires in the distance. By 3:00 a.m., firefighters were finally able to safely venture out and extinguish the firestorm. "East Youngstown early Saturday morning would inspire Dante to rewrite his Inferno," the *Vindicator* reported. The area of heaviest damage and destruction extended from the Sheet and Tube bridge, where the first shots were fired, north along the eastern side of Wilson Avenue to Tenth Street, including parts of Twelfth Street and much of Robinson Road.

Joseph Milgram, a telegrapher brought to the area from Pittsburgh to transmit reports to national news outlets, later recalled the scene that immediately greeted him as he arrived in East Youngstown on the trolley: "A whole block of stores was burned out. It had been bitter cold, and the

Looking toward Short Street from Wilson Avenue. *Courtesy of Thomas Molocea.*

Suspects in the custody of East Youngstown officials. *Courtesy of the Library of Congress.*

The ruins of Hamory Bank and a neighboring drugstore still smolder the day after a long night of arson. *Courtesy of Thomas Molocea.*

stores had icicles hanging on their fronts; cash registers, their money drawers missing, were scattered in the streets. We saw a large, ragged brick wall which, we were told, was a hospital under construction but had been dynamited. A bridge across the railroads to the steel mill had been dynamited, too, and was heavily guarded." In the days after, the *Vindicator* estimated that 25,000 people flooded the village to survey the damage.

Many if not most of the population of East Youngstown was made up of recent immigrants, and the *Vindicator* and other publications, with the partial exception of the *Youngstown Telegram*, went out of their way to blame "foreigners" or "foreign elements" for the confrontation on the bridge and the subsequent events. In many ways, this xenophobia prefigured the rise of the Ku Klux Klan in the Mahoning Valley, an era that began four short years after the riot.

On the morning of Saturday, January 8, a state militia force two thousand strong began arriving in East Youngstown. An order closing local saloons was extended to include all of Youngstown, Niles and Girard. Locals lamented that the order to close the saloons in East Youngstown was delayed until late Friday afternoon. In the aftermath of the blaze, police in the village "raided nearly every house in East Youngstown," the *Vindicator* reported.

Hundreds of shots had been fired, and after twelve hours of rioting, three people had been killed and over one hundred injured. Police arrested at least three hundred people in connection with the riot. Total damage was estimated at $1.5 million.

A grand jury was empaneled to investigate the causes of the riot and determine the responsible parties. Reporting in March 1916, it found nothing to substantiate claims that foreign provocateurs or agents of the Austro-Hungarian Empire had been involved in the strike or subsequent violence, as had been rumored. Several individuals were indicted for crimes committed on the night of the riot. Amazingly, the grand jury also held the Youngstown Sheet and Tube Company responsible for acts leading to the violence. It indicted numerous officials from various steel companies for violating the Valentine Anti-Trust Act. The grand jury also censured the mayor of East Youngstown, several members of the council and the police force. The officials were labeled as incompetent and unfit for office. Working-class men made up the bulk of the grand jury, but state judge W.H. Anderson overturned the indictments against the companies and municipal officials a few weeks later.

Curiosity seekers came from miles around to survey the damage in East Youngstown. *Courtesy of Thomas Molocea.*

In the end, the workers received a two-and-a-half-cent-an-hour raise, short of their demands. "It is noteworthy, however," the *American Labor Year Book* pointed out, "the increase forced by the strikers in Youngstown spread to the entire steel industry. "According to Sherry Lee Linkon and John Russo in *Steeltown U.S.A.: Work and Memory in Youngstown*, "The immediate result was an increase in wages, but the strike also contributed to the rise of what is often termed 'welfare capitalism' and the 'American Plan,' meaning greater attention to quality of life and a call for new forms of worker-management cooperation."

Sheet and Tube began publishing the *Bulletin* newsletter in 1919, one of the first of its kind. It contained feature articles on workers and their accomplishments, gossip and articles meant to cement bonds between the company and workers. More substantively, the company began to focus on the housing problem in East Youngstown and in neighboring Struthers, forming the Buckeye Land Company in 1917. Several tracts of housing were built in Struthers, as well as a unique series of structures in East Youngstown.

Blackburn Plat, as it came to be called, was one of the early uses of precast concrete homes. Covering forty acres off Robinson Road, not far from the epicenter of the 1916 riot, the rental units were occupied by immigrants and African Americans. The company-owned units served to correct the housing problem that helped lead to the explosion in early January. However, it also allowed Sheet and Tube to "gain control over workers," as Linkon and Russo point out. Even more important to the company, it allowed Sheet and Tube to compete for government war contracts, which were now only awarded to communities that offered appropriate worker housing.

Local municipal officials had different worries. After the riot, the unsavory reputation that the name *East Youngstown* carried troubled Youngstown's city fathers. The fact that East Youngstown was not actually part of the city itself seemed like a distinction that few outside the area would make, or so politicians in Youngstown thought. According to the *Vindicator*, the city fathers held that East Youngstown had two options: agree to be annexed, or change the village's name. "If East Youngstown opposes annexation, then for heaven's sake let the officials change its name," an unnamed city official told the *Vindicator*. "This outrage is a disgrace on the fair name of Youngstown. We want the rest of the country to know that the city of Youngstown is not directly concerned in this affair."

In 1926, Youngstown's politicians got their wish when East Youngstown became the city of Campbell, named after Sheet and Tube president James Campbell. The city's reputation remained tainted by the strike, however, and Campbell became known as a tough blue-collar town. The memory of the strike was immortalized in art, as well. Painter and muralist William Gropper famously depicted the conflict in his 1937 painting *Youngstown Strike*. That same a year, a new generation of steelworkers once again sought union recognition and better standards of living in another violent labor conflict, the "Little Steel" strike of 1937.

8

THE GREAT STEEL STRIKE OF 1919

The year 1919 rocked the nation and especially the state of Ohio. During those twelve tumultuous months, one out of five workers in the country went out on strike—a strike wave without precedent in American history to that point. Ohio alone experienced 237 strikes. It represented a number not duplicated until the massive strike wave of the late 1930s. From the bloody "May Day Riots" in Cleveland between pro- and antisocialist forces to the violent clashes of the Willys-Overland strike in Toledo, the state remained on edge throughout the year. At the center was the nationwide steel strike, a prolonged and violent conflict that lasted from September 22, 1919, until 1920. As one of the nation's largest steel districts, Youngstown floated near the eye of the storm. Pulled once again into the maelstrom, the city and the valley experienced a vicious and bloody labor conflict for the second time in three years.

In some ways, the 1915–16 strike in Youngstown and the rioting in East Youngstown helped set off a wave of labor militancy nationwide. Frank Morrison, secretary of the American Federation of Labor (AFL), visited Youngstown during the perilous steel strike of 1915–16. He immediately saw the potential for organizing the steel industry—a long-sought goal for the nation's labor leaders. Several months later, Morrison visited East Pittsburgh during a violent strike involving Westinghouse. The strike soon spread, with workers marching on several mills in the Pittsburgh area, demanding the eight-hour workday. Just as in East Youngstown, several people died in the ensuing clashes between workers and troops in the borough of Braddock. Yet according to the AFL *Weekly Newsletter*, Morrison came away from Pittsburgh with the feeling that such strikes proved "too turbulent to be exploited by the AFL."

However, the steel industry represented a critical part of the equation for America's battered labor movement. At the beginning of the twentieth century, membership in unions stood at a mere 10 percent of the non-agricultural labor force, according to historian David Brody. "Employers resisted labor organization relentlessly, and for the most part, successfully," he writes. "They penned the trade unions into a narrow field: the railroads, the coal mines, construction, clothing, certain skilled occupations." Organizing the steel industry held the key to unionizing the entirety of the mass-production sector. According to Brody, labor organizers recognized that this heavy industry needed to be the main target.

It would not be easy. Early twentieth-century steelworkers seemed increasingly powerless in the face of enormous steel concerns (such as U.S. Steel). The once-powerful Amalgamated Association of Iron and Steel Workers, which represented skilled, primarily English-speaking workers, was broken by Andrew Carnegie in 1892 after a blood-spattered strike in Homestead, Pennsylvania. By 1903, it had been dislodged from mills across the heart of industrial America. The Amalgamated failed to break out of its attachment to craft unionism, a type of union formation based on organizing workers by craft or trade. When the bloody and important Pressed Steel Car strike of 1909 took place in McKees Rocks, Pennsylvania, it was the radical Industrial Workers of the World labor union—a group that advocated for syndicalism, or a system advocating ownership of the means of production by workers organized in industrial unions—that came to the aid of workers.

The plight of workers like those at the Pressed Steel Car Company was extreme even by the standards of the day, yet most steelworkers faced what can only be described as hellish conditions in the mills. In 1910, 30 percent of the labor force worked seven days a week, and 75 percent worked a twelve-hour day. In 1909, U.S. Steel announced an "open shop" policy, dealing another body blow to labor. Increasingly, "company unions," much despised by labor organizers, were proffered in place of any potential collective bargaining arrangements. The great steel barons promised to never accept labor unions and the "closed shop."

The coming of the Great War (1914–18) helped reverse labor's waning fortunes in the steel industry. With a prolonged conflict raging in Europe, steel companies in America were cut off from their traditional source of immigrant labor. Instead, they imported Black laborers from the Jim Crow

The bloody Pressed Steel Car strike in McKees Rocks, Pennsylvania, symbolizes the labor discontent that pervaded the country a decade before the 1919 strike wave. *Courtesy of the author.*

South, yet this could not make up for the shortfall. And African American workers proved to be less pliable than the steel barons had hoped. After the strikes in East Youngstown and East Pittsburgh in 1916, wages rose slightly. Steel companies also pursued "Americanization" campaigns, designed to subvert what they considered to be the foreign influences of socialism, unionism and syndicalism among their immigrant workforces.

Yet it was to be government intervention that, at least temporarily, changed the balance of power in the steel industry during the war. In 1917, President Woodrow Wilson spoke at the AFL convention, and his administration rebuked efforts by the steel companies to gain emergency powers to ban strikes. The National War Labor Board emerged to mediate issues between labor and industry. This and other new agencies proved to be a boon for workers, who were finally able to organize without fear of retribution. The war itself changed perceptions among laborers, according to historians Raymond Boryczka and Lorin Lee Cary. "Wartime propaganda—especially the notion that this was a war to make the world safe for democracy—led more than one worker to conclude that there should be economic as well as political democracy within the U.S. By the fall of 1918 the quest for industrial democracy was well underway."

Workers were to be disappointed. After the armistice in November 1918, the government ended the agencies responsible for so many of labor's gains, and the prerogatives of management and the dreaded "open shop" policy returned in force. Yet in the summer of 1918, months before the war ended, the National Committee for Organizing Iron and Steel Workers had been created at a meeting of thirty union leaders in Chicago. They elected John Fitzpatrick of the Chicago Federation of Labor as temporary chairman. A former member of the radical IWW, William Z. Foster, served as secretary-treasurer. Foster's talents for organizing workers in Chicago, and his abilities at dealing with the numerous unions that made up the committee, appeared to make him the perfect candidate.

Two dozen craft unions eventually became part of the committee. Still operating under the idea of craft and not industrial unionism, the many unions involved represented workers in various parts of the skilled labor force. The Mine, Mill and Smelter Workers, along with the Iron, Steel, and Tin Workers, represented most of the unskilled workers. They found a ready audience, perhaps too ready for their timetable, among the mass of steelworkers suffering under a triumvirate of low pay, inflation and long, brutal workweeks.

Sheet and Tube workers load shrapnel cases, circa 1918. The war buoyed labor's power and increased expectations of workplace democracy. *Courtesy of the National Archives and Records Administration.*

Laborers of the Youngstown Sheet and Tube Company, circa 1919. According to David Brody, in 1919, the twelve-hour day was more common in the steel industry than it had been in 1911. *Courtesy of the National Archives and Records Administration.*

In a report released later during the strike itself, the Interchurch World Movement described the appalling conditions in Youngstown's mills, including twelve-hour workdays, low pay and shifts with no time for breaks or even lunch. Using one department as an example, the report vividly depicted the toll on the men: "So many men gave out under the strain and had to be fired for not being able to do the work…and the timekeeper begged the foreman not to discharge so many. There were about 100 men in the department, and about 35 to 50 were hired and fired each month." According to Boryczka and Cary, during a yearlong drive, union organizers signed up over 150,000 members across the country, with 30 percent of those coming from mills in Ohio. "The Cleveland and Youngstown districts proved especially fertile recruitment areas," they write. "Eight hours and the union" became the rallying cry for what would eventually become the "Great Steel Strike."

Companies responded to organizing drives by firing union activists and those suspected of union sympathies by the hundreds. In the Pittsburgh area, union organizers and workers were denied the right to assemble by local authorities. Pressure to strike began to build. In the summer of 1919, Fitzpatrick, Foster and D.J. Davis of the National Committee requested a meeting with Judge Elbert Gary, the powerful chairman of U.S. Steel. Gary refused to meet with the men. Gary's power was such that he spoke for most of the steel industry itself. In a last-ditch effort to avoid a strike, President Wilson asked union representatives to postpone any action until the October 6 industrial conference on issues in postwar industry.

The unions, however, started something they could not control. A strike date had been set for September 22, and the men were in no mood to wait. In *Savage Peace: Hope and Fear in America, 1919*, Ann Hagedorn describes how workers in Youngstown represented the desire to commence with the strike, even against the judgement of the National Committee: "The leaders of the Youngstown workers, for example, during the week after the strike date was set, sent a telegram to the National Committee, in the tone of a warning. The A.F.L. must stick to the September 22 date or 'the men will strike regardless of any postponement, and we will lose control of the situation.'"

On September 23, men began streaming out of the mills in Youngstown and Warren. There is disagreement over how many men nationally went on strike. Secretary Foster later claimed in his book that a total of 365,000 struck, with 70,000 workers in total going out in East Youngstown, Youngstown, Struthers, Hubbard, Niles, Canton, Alliance, Massillon, Warren, Farrell, New Castle, Sharon and Butler. David Brody puts the national number closer to 250,000, or half of the total steel workforce.

Fearing a repeat of the violence of 1916, Mayor T.J. McVey of East Youngstown ordered 20 special officers to be appointed to the police force. Officials in Struthers announced plans to recruit 125 special deputies. But violence first broke out across the border in New Castle, Pennsylvania. Seven men and two women were shot in what the *Youngstown Vindicator* described as a "riot." In addition, 2 policemen were assaulted by a crowd (1 officer was stabbed and the other hit with a brick) that refused to allow workers to enter the Shenango and Greer plants of the American Sheet and Tin Plate Company. The fight followed the appearance of several hundred men said to be from Youngstown.

Two men were also killed and several hundred injured during prolonged clashes in Farrell, Pennsylvania. The *Vindicator* reported thousands of "foreigners" chanting "Bolsheviki" (a reference to the Russian Bolsheviks) as they marched through the town. It is important to remember that the *Vindicator* and many other papers at the time tended to blame disturbances during the riots on immigrants and "Red" sympathizers (often without direct evidence). The Russian Revolution had occurred two years earlier, and the first "Red Scare" was spreading across the country. Union organizers continually contended with charges that strikers—and the unions

Plants such as this Sheet and Tube mill emptied out after the steel strike began on September 22. *Courtesy of the National Archives and Records Administration.*

themselves—were compromised by communists and/or anarchists. Such tensions proved especially potent in Ohio, which saw more voters cast their ballots for socialists in 1910 than any other state in the country.

While making stern distinctions between "Americans" and "foreigners," the *Vindicator* acknowledged that within days the mills were "crippled" by the walkout of machinists, electricians and railroad employees in the mill yards. Secretary Foster later corroborated that reporting in his book: "In the immediate Youngstown district the strike was highly effective, hardly a ton of steel being produced anywhere for several weeks. This was due largely to the walkout of the railroad men employed in the mill yards, who acted of their own volition."

In Trumbull County, fabricating plants closed as the pool of unskilled labor dried up due to the strike. By the night of September 23, the Trumbull County Steel Company had closed its Warren plants. The *Vindicator* claimed a total of 42,700 on strike in the Youngstown district. A total of only 25,000 were reported idle in Cleveland. Another person was killed and six injured in Farrell on the night of September 23, but for the time being, Youngstown remained "the only quiet district," the *Vindicator* reported.

Within a short period of time, workers, facing the possibility of a long strike, began to rein in their spending. Butchers and retailers selling meat reported a drop-off in business. Some local establishments tried to find ways to accommodate the out-of-work steelmen. Dr. E.W. Roth of West Federal Street offered dental services with fees not due until after the strike. S. Levin and Son clothiers on South Watt Street offered deep discounts during a "Striker's Sale." Advertisements encouraging idled workers to come to the Hotel Ohio to inquire about learning how to sell real estate appeared in the *Vindicator*. Still, workers at the local mills received paychecks at month's end for wages for the first half of September. Desperation had not arrived.

As the steel industry ramped up its campaign to place blame for the strike at the feet of recent immigrants and "radical elements," support did emerge for the strikers. Editorials appearing in the *Vindicator* and the *Youngstown Telegram* with titles such as "Foreign Born Not to Blame" provided some contrast to the message proffered by industry. The Cosmopolitan Press Club, an organization of valley foreign-language newspapers, published messages denouncing xenophobic rhetoric, which they said attempted to blame recent arrivals for violence and labor unrest. At the end of September, the

The walkout of railroad men greatly aided the strikers' quest to shut down steel production in Youngstown. *Courtesy of the National Archives and Records Administration.*

Mahoning County United Labor Congress voiced its unequivocal support for the strikers and against industry rhetoric targeting foreign-born workers. A similar war of words played out in steel communities across the country.

On September 29, the *Telegram* reported that none of the valley steel companies would comment on how long they thought the strike could last. *Iron Age*, an industry publication, claimed that workers in Buffalo were beginning to come back to the mills. Yet no movement proved visible in the valley: "Cleveland and the Mahoning Valley remain the most affected points. Virtually every plant in those territories is idle," *Iron Age* reported. Apparently, in reaction to the potential of a long strike, foreign-born workers began to slowly migrate out of the area. According to the *Telegram*, nearly 150 a day were leaving Youngstown by the end of the month.

At the end of September, workers began returning to the American Sheet and Tin Plate Company in Farrell. The *Telegram* reported that this development had affected the attitudes of workers, who eventually began to return to the Ohio Works in Youngstown. Two hundred "American-born men" voted to return to the Ohio Works at the end of the month, and management reported enough men on hand to possibly start two idled blast furnaces. Partially in reaction to these developments, the AFL held a rally in Lincoln Park that attracted five hundred strikers. John McCadden, Youngstown district secretary, sought to dispel any "whispers of defeat" and insisted the strike remained eminently winnable, the *Vindicator* reported.

On October 6, the much-heralded industrial conference began at the Pan-American building in Washington, D.C. Three different groups were present (a public, a labor and an employer group) to try to form a framework for the governing of peaceful industrial relations between labor and industry, with the public representing the third part of the equation. The labor group put forward a resolution calling for the recognition of workers to organize themselves in labor unions, to bargain collectively for wages and to be represented by arbiters of their choosing during negotiations with management. Over the next few weeks, deliberations at the congress played out against the backdrop of the strike.

As the industrial conference began, long lines of picketers descended on the entrances of the East Youngstown plant of Youngstown Sheet and Tube and the Ohio Works. So many striking workers amassed at the Division Street entrance of the Ohio Works that "it became apparent that there would be no attempt to operate the plant," according to the *Telegram*. However, by October 9, a group of strikers voted to return to work at a meeting held at the Warren Opera House. The Trumbull Steel Company refused to

On October 9, the Trumbull Steel Company reported that strikers were ready to return to work. *Courtesy of the author.*

furnish any numbers, but it was clear that the situation was moving toward management's side in Warren.

In his 1920 book, Secretary Foster claimed that "armies of scabs were poured" into the Youngstown district in a bid to keep the mills running. This led to numerous confrontations between strikers and the men brought to the area to keep the plants working. One such confrontation turned deadly in early October. According to the *Vindicator*, a group of foreign strikers confronted African American workers (who were often recruited from the South, sometimes under false pretenses, by steel companies to act as strikebreakers) coming out of the Hubbard plant of Youngstown Sheet and Tube. The workers headed for the Erie Railroad tracks with the strikers on their heels. Somewhere near the Lake Shore depot, one of the workers turned and fired at the strikers, killing one man and injuring several others. It was the first but not the last casualty of the strike in Mahoning Valley.

On October 9, the Brier Hill Steel Company blew in one of its blast furnaces, the first to be restarted in the valley since the strike began. The East Youngstown plant of Sheet and Tube fired up its number two stack on the same day. By the beginning of the fourth week of the strike, enough men had returned to Trumbull Steel to allow the company to announce plans to soon be fully operational. Members of the Amalgamated Association of Iron, Steel, and Tin Workers came to an individual agreement with the plants of the Empire, Thomas, Western Reserve, Deforest and Mahoning Valley Steel companies.

On October 23, the industrial conference ended with a defeat of the resolution concerning union recognition. In a letter to the conference shortly before it adjourned, President Wilson wrote: "At a time when the nations of the world are endeavoring to find a way of avoiding international war, are we to confess that there is no method to be found for carrying on industry except in the spirit and with the very methods of war?" The events of the steel strike itself seemed to give Wilson his answer. On October 14 in Brier Hill, a man was shot by a police officer when constables and strikers clashed. The night before, a "near riot," as the *Vindicator* described it, broke out on the Center Street Bridge. In Canton, the state militia mobilized in response to reports of rioting in the city. In Gary, Indiana, the steel city named after Elbert Gary himself, federal troops occupied the environs and martial law was declared. The industrial war continued unabated.

As the strike turned against the workers, violence seemed to accelerate. A group of Youngstown men was imprisoned for being part of a conspiracy to burn the homes of strikebreakers. Replacement workers were pulled from streetcars going to the Ohio Works and beaten. Serious shoot-outs between police and strikers occurred in places such as Steelton and Poland Avenue. As events progressed, women increasingly came to the picket lines and even fought replacement workers, company guards and local police. A group of twenty-three women from Struthers, the wives of striking steelworkers, descended on local police outside Stop 14 on Poland Avenue. The officers described them as "infuriating amazons who fought tooth and nail against them." According to the *Vindicator*, the women dared the police to shoot them as they fought and yelled: "Me men no work. You scabbage!" Armed with a mixture of red pepper, cayenne and salt, some of the women temporarily blinded many of the officers after throwing the concoction in their faces. After that incident, officers began wearing gas masks when called to disturbances on Poland Avenue.

November witnessed a variety of violent disturbances around the city as tensions heightened. On November 7, plants across Youngstown reported serious trouble. Mounted officers and reserve police were dispatched to all the mills as pitched battles and shoot-outs were reported. As more men reported back to work and more mills began to operate again, the confrontations grew more violent. Striker Joe Gradulich was stabbed in the neck during a fight with a neighbor who had returned to the Ohio Works plant. Some foreign-born workers, who ironically had often been blamed for being a driving force behind the strike itself, now found themselves under attack for crossing the picket line.

After the murder of striker Gabriel Zitnjak in late November, 1,500 steelmen marched in his funeral procession, which covered six miles from East Youngstown to Calvary Cemetery on the west side of Youngstown. The event made the front page in papers as far away as Washington, D.C., and North Carolina. Fred Pachen, an employee of Carnegie Steel, became the third and last man to die during the strike. He was beaten unconscious at the corner of Ardale Street and West Rayen Avenue before later stumbling onto the Erie Railroad tracks, where he was found. He died in the hospital in mid-December.

On November 17, famed journalist and activist Mary Heaton Vorse was spotted among the thousands of strikers and supporters who descended on Wilson and Poland Avenues to join the pickets. Vorse, whose work appeared in national publications including the *Atlantic*, *McClure's* and the *New Republic*, put her Youngstown reporting into an article, "Behind the Picket Line: The Story of a Slovak Steel Striker—How He Lives and Thinks." Vorse had been invited by one of the picketers to meet his wife and eight children at their home in a neighborhood that she described as "the most meritorious community, from the point of view of decency, that I have seen in any steel town." The man's wife explained, "They only get to know their papa now, since the strike. When father works fourteen hours night and ten light, he never sees the children." In the article's close, Vorse evocatively described the world she had visited during the strike: "The mills are as beautiful as a volcanic convulsion. The great chimneys follow one another like the pipes of a black organ, and from these chimneys belches forth a mighty symphony of smoke. But in the foreground you will see sights every day in the streets of the steel towns that will wring your heart."

Many of these families made it through long months of the strike by a combination of thriftiness and aid from national strike headquarters in Pittsburgh. The *Vindicator* claimed that foreign-born workers were better prepared for the strike, with money saved and Liberty Bonds to draw from, comparing them favorably (in a marked change of pace) to the wives of native-born American workers: "The modern American wife, especially if she is young, spends four or five times as much for clothing as the foreign-born wife. To keep up with Dame Fashion is the ambition of many a woman and nobody denies that it costs a pretty penny." This was assuredly an exaggeration, however.

A commissary for striking workers opened on East Boardman Street in downtown in October. Ration cards were issued to families of six or more (not an uncommon size at the time). During the first half of the week, families received ten pounds of potatoes; five pounds of bread; one can each of tomatoes, corn, peas and navy beans; one pound of coffee; and a can of milk. During the second half of the week, the same groceries were issued except for salted meat instead of bacon, red beans instead of navy beans and no coffee. By mid-November, the commissary department claimed it could feed approximately ten thousand families in the Youngstown district.

Throughout the strike, local clergy supported the strikers. While this also proved to be the case in tough steel towns like Braddock, Pennsylvania (where "labor priest" Reverend Adalbert Kazinczy provided enormous spiritual support to the union), it was far from the norm in many steel districts, as Boryczka and Cary emphasize. They describe how local officials in the Youngstown district overwhelmingly supported the steel companies and acted to arrest organizers. Most importantly, local authorities imperiled their ability to organize. East Youngstown authorities arrested John E. McCadden, secretary-treasurer for the Youngstown District of the National Committee, and two of his aides after they addressed a meeting of strikers. They were charged with "criminal syndicalism." In Youngstown, Mayor A.W. Craver issued a ban on all meetings in which any matters involving the steel strike were to be discussed. He also attempted to enforce a prohibition on crowds gathering on public streets. The order held until almost the end of the year, when the strike was all but broken.

Secretary Foster of the National Committee visited Youngstown three times during the strike. A committee of local businessmen soon asked Mayor Craver to keep him away from the city. Petitions from an unknown source circulated in the city, calling for leaders of the strike from outside of the area to leave. Organizers at strike headquarters publicly rebuked the petitions and vowed to stay on. However, much to their chagrin, the strike itself got caught up in the seemingly endless publicity surrounding labor radicals, anarchists and most especially communist influence in the labor movement—and even in the Federal Trade Commission—all of which represented a kind of precursor to the post–World War II Red Scare and the emergence of McCarthyism. The combined impact helped to further weaken support for the strike.

After the outbreak of the national coal strike in November, newspapers began to devote less coverage to the steel strike. Approximately forty thousand Ohio coal workers walked off the job, and suddenly the prospect of a coal shortage that would massively impact basic industry—along with the ability of people to heat their homes—seemed to be the most important labor issue facing the nation. While this new drama played out, men across the country continued to drift back into the mills. Effectively, the strike seemed all but broken in Youngstown, though it did not officially end until the beginning of January.

In *Pittsburgh and the Great Steel Strike of 1919*, Ryan C. Brown describes Mary Vorse's encounters with desperate strikers (who pleaded with her to reassure them) at the National Committee headquarters in Youngstown as the strike neared its end: "The steelworkers' sobbing in the dark hall outside the National Committee Office in Youngstown will always be to me the sound of the dying strike."

After the failure of the 1919 strike, it would not be until many years later— with the passage of the Wagner Act in 1935 and the coming of World War II—that the union movement recovered. Yet Brown credits the 1919 strike as a precursor to the successful organizing efforts in the steel industry in Youngstown and elsewhere in the 1930s and '40s. "I think it's worth thinking of the Great Steel Strike, while it was a failure, as the first kernel of victory for the industrial labor movement."

9

"Worker's Colony" Survives as Testament
to Housing and Labor History

Industrialism, the main creative force of the nineteenth century, produced the most
degraded urban environment the world had yet seen.
—Lewis Mumford

It would be difficult, if not impossible, to describe to a young person today the polluted and smog-ridden environment that was the world surrounding the steel mills of the Mahoning Valley, especially in the time before modern pollution controls. It would be just as difficult to describe to almost anyone living today the sheer scale of the degradation of East Youngstown (and communities like it) during the early twentieth century: shabby hovels without even the pretense of livability filled with overworked men and large families. This is the environment the Industrial Revolution produced for so many laborers. And such conditions played a key role in the 1916 riot that destroyed much of the village's business district.

Once the flames died down after the 1916 strike, and before the national steel strike of 1919 began, the Youngstown Sheet and Tube Company inaugurated a new chapter in local housing history. Fearing more militant worker discontent, as well as further unionization drives, the company formed a subsidiary called the Buckeye Land Company in 1917 to finance the first of four housing plats for the company's workers. Construction of the first plat, Blackburn—a place that would become notable in both local and national history—took place from 1918 through 1920.

Blackburn Plat under construction, circa 1919. *Courtesy of Timothy Sokoloff.*

According to a 1918 article in *The American Architect*, a great deal of thought went into the initial preparations on the forty-acre site situated off Robinson Road less than a half mile uphill from Wilson Avenue in East Youngstown (modern-day Campbell):

> *Before deciding on their design and construction in this East Youngstown Colony, the Buckeye Land Company went into a very careful survey of local conditions and into an extended study of what has already been done elsewhere under similar circumstances. The result was that they adopted three or four-room houses with a lawn in front and a garden and service lane in the rear, the construction to be fireproof and permanent, of reinforced concrete, unit method.*

One of the most notable aspects of the Blackburn plat units was the use of precast concrete building elements. At the time, the use of reinforced concrete was still relatively new. Incidentally, Julius Kahn, who devised one of the most revolutionary systems in the world for using reinforced concrete, lived and worked in Youngstown in 1917. Yet the Blackburn development and units were designed by Conzelman, Herding and Boyd (under the guidance of Franz Herding, Swiss architect and city planner) and constructed by the Unit Construction Company, both St. Louis firms. A 1918 article in *Engineering News-Record* noted that in the Blackburn project "precast slabs, poured in a yard and erected by a traveler [derrick], are being used for the first time in this country to construct dwelling-houses."

Built on land sold to Sheet and Tube by the heirs of Silas Blackburn, the "worker's colony," as it was sometimes called, consisted of 281 units of

New residents occupy homes while construction continues in Blackburn Plat, circa 1920. *Courtesy of Timothy Sokoloff.*

row housing. The units had a depth of two rooms, allowing adequate light into the quarters. Each unit included a basement with a shower complete with a separate entrance. This unique design element accommodated mill workers who needed to bathe immediately after arriving at home. Water, heat and electricity were included. Wooden stairs led to the second-floor bathrooms, and Mediterranean-style red titles covered the roofs. According to Youngstown Sheet and Tube's *Bulletin* newsletter, in 1922, rents ranged from twelve to seventeen dollars a month. Units with coal-burning stoves rented from fifteen to twenty-one dollars a month. The company stated that approximately 250 families lived at Blackburn in 1920.

Compared to what was available to laborers in much of the Youngstown area, these units proved to be a fantastic upgrade. *Engineering News-Record* referred to Blackburn as "one of the first attempts to provide living quarters of a permanent and inexpensive type, which will be comfortable, sanitary and practically fireproof." Advertisements by the Buckeye Land Company called Blackburn "a good place to bring up your children to be real Americans."

Blackburn was specifically designed to accommodate "foreign" workers—who had yet to prove their "Americanness" to the company— and Black workers. African Americans were segregated from the European immigrants within the colony. Streets in the African American section were named after Black luminaries: Booker Avenue, for Booker T. Washington, and Douglas Drive, for Frederick Douglass. The company advertised two-, three- and four-room units for rent in the "colored" section, which encompassed 135 units.

The nature of the setting was designed to be of a country-like character. A "public square," playground and wading pool rounded out the amenities.

A funeral procession passes through the African American section of the worker homes, circa 1924. *Courtesy of Timothy Sokoloff.*

Sheet and Tube opened one of its four company stores on-site for workers to shop at. The custom of taking in boarders, commonplace among many immigrant families, was strictly forbidden by the Buckeye Land Company. The company, and indeed many of the publications that wrote about the development, saw all of the above as means to encourage "American family values" among "alien employees," as the *American Architect* described them. Writers for the *Bulletin*, a Sheet and Tube company publication, echoed those same sentiments in their coverage of Blackburn and other plats of company housing.

Units at Blackburn were only available for rent. The next plat of housing developed by the Buckeye Land Company, Highview, located in Struthers, offered detached homes for rent or sale to "foreign born employees of the company who have made themselves valuable employees in the mill," as the *Bulletin* put it. The third plat—Loveland Farms, located near the Youngstown border with Struthers—offered detached homes for sale to management and skilled white workers born in America. The company eventually built a fourth plat called Overlook in Struthers. Only American-born whites could rent duplexes in Overlook. (In later years, Paul C. Kuegle, manager of the Buckeye Land Company, told the *American Iron and Steel Institute* that company housing for industrial workers ultimately proved more crucial for renters than for those looking to purchase a home.)

Sheet and Tube decided to cease construction at Blackburn in the early 1920s, despite having nearby land available. According to historian Donna DeBlasio, the severe recession of 1920–21, among other things, may have led to this decision. The company did, however, consider the project—along with a similar venture erecting precast concrete housing for coal workers in Nemacolin, Pennsylvania, built through another subsidiary, the Buckeye Coal Company—to be a success. Youngstown Sheet and Tube architect Barton E. Brooke told the *American Concrete Institute* in 1922 that "it is a paying investment to build modern houses, no matter what class of people are to occupy them, or to what they have been formally accustomed."

As part of its overall approach to what historians often refer to as "welfare capitalism," Sheet and Tube also offered a variety of leisure and recreational activities for workers living in Blackburn. The company held an annual field day at Campbell Park, with games for the children and a dance hall for the adults. The company turned an old slag heap into a baseball field for the workers, another leisure activity viewed as being properly American. In 1921, Sheet and Tube's athletic and recreation committee fielded a team in the City Federation League.

After the onset of the Great Depression, the company again became involved in attempting to ameliorate the dire conditions facing workers as economic conditions worsened. At one point in the early 1930s, Sheet and Tube's mills operated at less than 20 percent capacity. As the national unemployment rate climbed toward 25 percent in 1932, employee representatives helped persuade the company to turn over vacant land for workers to plant food. The company extended credit for seeds and plants. Company supervisors guided everything from care and maintenance of the soil to basic methods of canning. Blackburn residents grew food on twenty-eight acres of adjoining gardens in 1932. Sheet and Tube estimated that there were approximately one thousand employee gardens in 1933. A joint committee of employees and company representatives adopted a relief plan to offer credit at the employees' cooperatives stores for those who needed help obtaining groceries. According to DeBlasio, the company eventually decreased the rent on units at Blackburn during the Depression to between $7.00 to $13.25 a month, with a $2.00 charge for a garage, an option that first appeared in the late 1920s. Few workers, however, could afford cars.

In 1942, Sheet and Tube announced the dissolution of the Buckeye Land Company. John W. Galbreath, a Columbus real estate operator who would go on to become one of the richest men in America, bought the company housing in 1943. Two years earlier, Galbreath had purchased virtually the entirety of the Carnegie-Illinois Company's housing stock in the company town of McDonald in Trumbull County. He also bought the "Cement City" houses, an early experiment with poured-in-place concrete, in Donora, Pennsylvania. After Galbreath sold off the Blackburn homes, some individuals painted their units different colors and changed the interiors to suit their tastes. Yet, according to former resident and local historian Florence Galida, the community remained eminently livable.

All of that changed in the years after September 19, 1977, known as "Black Monday" in the Mahoning Valley. On that day, Sheet and Tube announced the imminent closing of the Campbell Works. The decision ultimately led to the loss of five thousand jobs and devastated the city's tax base. Many residents, including those in the old worker homes, left the area. "Our city was very family-oriented," Galida later told the *Vindicator*. "Families were ripped apart." In 1982, as Campbell and Youngstown were caught in a "regional depression," the Sheet and Tube company homes were added to the National Register of Historic Places.

Conditions in the community grew more challenging throughout the 1980s. In 1989, Joseph Stroney, a resident since 1942, bemoaned the state of many of the homes on Douglas Drive, originally located in the segregated African American section. "They're a mess," he told the *Vindicator*. "As soon as someone moves out, someone else comes by and rips out the wiring and plumbing. No one takes care of them." The fact that the row houses share walls made it difficult for the city to demolish heavily damaged vacant units located next to occupied units. Yet, in a true twist of fate, while the remains of the old company that built them fell to the wrecking ball, most of the worker homes continued to stand. Although Florence Galida and an older generation of Campbell residents championed the homes and helped them gain recognition as a historic site, the aging and battered community needed a new champion as a new century dawned. The job fell to Tim Sokoloff.

After growing up in Struthers, Sokoloff set off on his own in the late 1980s, moving into one of the company homes. He recalls marveling at the solid concrete walls and tiled roofs, but at the time, he did not know of their historical importance. He later moved out but returned to the community in 2007. Appropriately enough, he made his new home 40 Chambers Street, which once housed the office of the Buckeye Land Company. By then, Sokoloff had become aware of the history contained in the solid walls of concrete lining the old community. "That's when I began to understand the historical value of this place," he said. "Once I did start to find out the

The corner of Delmar Avenue and Chambers Street as it appeared in 2012. *Photo by the author.*

history, I realized that these [apartments] really are worth saving. It's not just their structure. It's their history, it's who we are. They're a monumental piece of American history."

The scale of the challenge soon became evident. "Nobody would come here in 2007," he said. "You couldn't even see the offices I live in now. This place was a wreck. All the grass was overgrown. The trees and brush went so high that you couldn't even see the sign that says, 'national historic site.'" He found abandoned cash registers, pay phones and other remnants of criminal activity strewn in the weeds. Gangs plagued the area. His unit was one of the few to have both windows and doors. Sokoloff feared that if he did not get a cleanup of the neighborhood jump-started, the city would attempt to demolish the rest of the units, of which 194 of the original 281 still stood.

Over a decade later, much has been accomplished, Sokoloff said. Crime has been greatly reduced, and neighbors no longer live in fear of criminal activity. Working with the community, donors and volunteers, he has helped renovate abandoned units that now house new tenants, cleared completely overgrown streets and renovated the last of the community's old archways. But vacant units, sometimes scorched by fire, and absentee landlords still haunt the community. Large sections, including much of the

A section of the company homes near Robinson Road as they appeared in 2021. *Photo by the author.*

Timothy Sokoloff is leading the charge to preserve the homes for future generations. *Photo by the author.*

formerly segregated area reserved for African Americans, are empty and in danger of being demolished.

The battered worker homes, however, still garner plenty of attention and have turned into a tourist and media attraction of sorts. "We've had literally hundreds of people come here to see the place," he explained. And though much work remains, Sokoloff hopes to put the old worker homes on track to see another hundred years of history.

10

The Evolution of Central Square

I n the summer of 2020, as the COVID-19 pandemic raged, I ventured to Central Square in downtown Youngstown. With most of the restaurant and entertainment venues closed, the stream of traffic that usually creates a cacophony of noise proved to be almost nonexistent. Hundreds of birds perched on the islands in the middle of the square chirped together in unison, creating a somewhat surreal harmony echoing off the buildings. I walked across from East Federal Street into the middle of the islands and looked up at the city's Civil War Soldiers Monument, affectionately referred to as the "Man on the Monument." The monument must have looked much the same to me as it had to those who witnessed its dedication in 1870. The same cannot be said for the rest of the square. It has been years since Federal Plaza has been dismantled and longer still since trolleys and busses made the square a central transportation hub and a site for rallies and political speechmaking. Change has been a constant in Central Square.

Looking back in 1924, Realty Trust Company employee W.B. Hall described a very different square in the pages of the *Vindicator*. The Man on the Monument remained the only enduring focal point he recognized from the square of his youth:

> *To look at Central Square as it appears under the pitiless glare of an August sun one carries away no impression of a past that is crowded with legend. The only focusing point of tradition is a monument of a stiffly posed Civil War soldier, but the perspective is in the background of signs advertising*

the virtue of false teeth, dairy lunches, and cigarettes. Idlers straddle the ornamental cannon. Bits of campaign posters clutter up the street. There is the din of rumbling tracks and changing trolleys. The crowds flow through the square like a lazy river. This is the realism of Central Square.

Hall's impressions of Central Square as it appeared during downtown's height in the 1920s are laced with nostalgia for the old "Diamond," as the square was once called. Indeed, many historical remembrances of the city center from the early and mid-twentieth century carry more than a whiff of nostalgia for "simpler times." Yet the square itself has been called by many different names, appeared in many different forms, served many different purposes and left many different impressions from 1802 to the present day.

In the late 1790s, the state of Connecticut sold part of the Western Reserve to the Connecticut Land Company. An enterprising New Yorker named John Young purchased "Township Number Two" in the second range from the company in 1797. The authors of *Mahoning Memories* contend that Young probably first arrived in 1796 to inspect the land before agreeing to the sale. Young and a group that likely included Isaac Powers, Phineas Hill and Daniel Shehy first landed at what later became known as Spring Common. They apparently met up with the first settler in the area, James Hillman, who would play an important role in the settlement.

The early settlement's nucleus took shape in the floodplain close to the Mahoning River. "If you look at the geographic center of Youngstown Township, it's roughly where Oak Hill Cemetery is," said Bill Lawson, head of the Mahoning Valley Historical Society. "And I think we all can agree that would not be a good location for a village or a central business district." It is likely that a central settlement situated near the river would have been advantageous in terms of transportation and possibly for defense. Early settlers and census takers arrived by canoe on the Mahoning River, sometimes sounding a horn to announce their arrival.

The original town plat of 1802, laid out by Young, has the town square (measuring 250 by 400 feet) in the center of a standard grid pattern of the kind that prevailed throughout the Connecticut Western Reserve. At the time, the square would have resembled a village green or commons, likely with grazing animals in the vicinity. Somewhere between 1802 and 1804, settlers erected a one-story school made from logs on the square. Anywhere from twenty to forty students attended in the early years. Another larger school, called the "Academy" by the locals, emerged on the corner of the square in the early 1820s. As early as 1811, Youngstowners referred to the

NORTH

Wood Street   66 feet   wide

wide   300 feet   wide   Street   wide   wide

Wick   Street   43 feet   wide

43 feet   300 feet   66 feet   150 feet   wide   Central Square   66 feet   43 feet

150 feet   300 feet   226 feet   226 feet   300 feet   150 feet

Federal   100 feet   wide   Street

Street   300 feet   Street   250 X 400 feet   150 feet   100 feet   Street   Street

Boardman   Street   43 feet   wide

Hazel   300 feet   Phelps   Market   Champion   Walnut

Front   Street   66 feet   wide

SOUTH

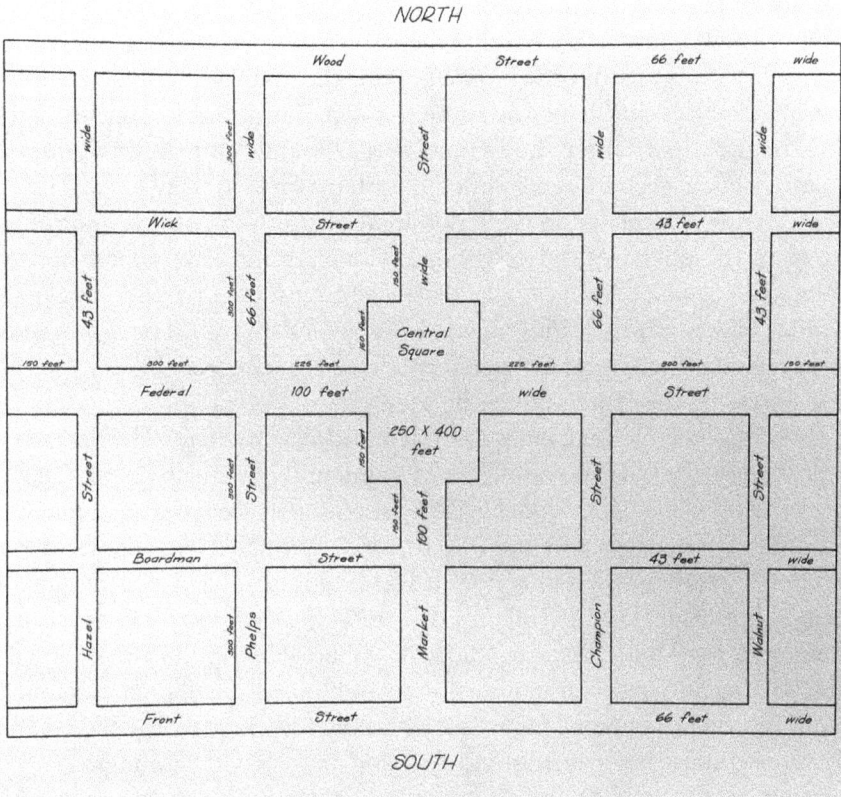

The original 1802 plat of Central Square and surrounding environs. *Courtesy of the author.*

square as the "Diamond." The origins of the name are unclear, though it is possible that if you look at the square in the right way, a diamond can be visualized. In later years, a business block named after the Diamond emerged off the square.

For decades, the square was known for its poor drainage and even swampy appearance. During heavy rains, ducks routinely made a pond in the square their home. A plank allowed pedestrians to walk across the widest part of the muck. In the twentieth century, journalist Clingan Jackson looked back and juxtaposed the early swampy square with the contemporary square of the 1950s: "The first Youngstown children who found cattails in that pond for Fourth of July flares or sat on the banks to throw stones at frogs or turtles, probably never envisioned that someday the towers of a skyscraper age might even dim the light there."

Early Youngstowners unceremoniously came to use the square as the town dump as well, filling in some of the marshier parts with ashes, cinders and other refuse. Despite this, the square became the main attraction for the early traveling circuses that regularly came to town. This tradition persisted until the arrival of ever-larger shows (and new buildings and traffic around the square) encouraged circuses to pitch their tents farther away toward lots off West Avenue. Private residences dominated early downtown Youngstown, but commercial, civic and religious buildings gradually emerged in and around the square as well. First Baptist Church served parishioners on the square. The first post office opened on the Diamond. The Youngstown Hotel served weary travelers, who were sure to find a ready hitching post for their horses, as they surrounded the square.

Many nineteenth and early twentieth-century residents considered the dedication of the Civil War Soldiers Monument the first step in truly shaping the character of the Diamond. Civil War monuments began going up in Ohio within the first two years of the war. In 1863, Bristolville erected a stone urn to honor local men killed in action. It was Ohio's first Civil War monument. Former governor David Tod (himself a Youngstowner) first proposed a monument for Youngstown in 1864. A public subscription drive aimed to raise the funds to build a monument, but with only a small population in the township, it fell to some of the wealthier families to make up the shortfall.

The original cornerstone stood ready to be placed in Youngstown's old cemetery near Wood Street. However, plans for a new courthouse at that location ultimately caused the monument project to be moved to Central Square. Two future presidents, Representative James Garfield and Governor Rutherford B. Hayes, appeared for the dedication and unveiling in 1870. The forty-seven-foot-high monument erected that day consists of a granite shaft topped with a soldier dressed in a private's uniform. The bearded private, with an overcoat thrown over his shoulder, stands with his hand on his gun at "parade rest." The "soldier at parade rest" became a commonplace element of Civil War monument design across the North. For example, a very similar monument can be seen in Painesville, Ohio. After approximately 1889, this style spread to the monuments being built to honor Confederate soldiers in the South.

In panels near the base of the monument are the names of the 111 men from Youngstown who died in the conflict. Below that, an inscription reads, "Erected by the citizens of Youngstown in memory of the heroes of the township who gave their lives to their country in the war of the Rebellion, 1861 to 1865." The original soldier fell from his perch and was decapitated in 1951. In 1955, Bertolini Brothers of Youngstown replaced him with the marble statue you see today. In the early 1870s, two Civil War–era cannons were placed next to the Man on the Monument. The cannons were originally meant for Fort Sumter, where the Civil War began in April 1861.

In the decades after the dedication of the Civil War Soldiers Monument, the area around Central Square began to change, slowly at first, then rapidly as the early twentieth century unfolded. Transportation changed after a franchise was given to the Youngstown Street Railway Company to run a horse-drawn streetcar line in the mid-1870s. The county seat moved to Youngstown in 1876. Paved streets and electric lighting downtown followed in the 1880s as the city began curbing the south side of the square. This led the Second National Bank to erect a building on the northeast corner. In 1874, Youngstown's entertainment options took a quantum leap with the opening of the Grand Opera House on the southwest corner of the square. The new performance venue attracted road shows and repertoire opera companies from across the country.

By 1889, the two islands in Central Square contained the Man on the Monument on the southern island and, to the north, a small pool with a rudimentary fountain made of blast iron slag. According to Lawson, "There was also a well that was dug, which fed the fountain, but people could use that as a common drinking well." But the square and downtown were poised for major changes as the new century dawned. In 1899, the Market Street Viaduct opened. This new route to the south side added more traffic to the already growing east–west flows passing through the square. In 1902, a streetcar loop was built around the square. This transformed Central Square into the city's main traffic hub. Electric streetcars serving the downtown and surrounding neighborhoods now landed in the heart of the city, as did the interurban streetcar lines, which took passengers to neighboring communities in the valley and western Pennsylvania. Ticket offices were located on the square, and the sight of passengers loading on and off the trollies became commonplace. Central Square entered a new stage in its evolution.

There proved to be some public resistance to the streetcar loop, and as the city center rapidly changed, Youngstowners pointed with pride to the garden-like nature of Central Square, perhaps as the last connection to the more bucolic downtown of the nineteenth century. In postcards and photos of the Diamond from the early nineteenth century, shade trees can be seen surrounding both islands of the square. The addition of a Victorian fountain in 1906 to the north island of the square added to the impression of Central Square as a kind of park. The $4,000 "Maid of the Mist," as it was known, was crowned by a small statue of a goddess. Initially white, it was later painted green by the city's Irish safety director. The *Vindicator* even created a weekly column in which the fountain and the Civil War statue came to life after midnight each night and "did the town." Clingan Jackson wrote the column for several years. A proposal to add a monument commemorating the Spanish-American War to join the monument and the fountain, while popular, never moved beyond the planning stage.

During the early 1900s, the area around Central Square was changing beyond all recognition. The old wooden structures of early downtown gave way to masonry buildings. Skyscrapers, the symbol of any true metropolis, began to materialize. The original Mahoning National Bank and the Second National Bank, while impressive by nineteenth-century building standards, were both less than five stories tall. The construction of the Dollar Bank Building in 1901 gave Central Square its first skyscraper and an entirely new appearance. It was joined in 1906 by the Stambaugh Building (designed by renowned Detroit architect Albert Kahn) and the Mahoning National Bank (also by Kahn) in 1910.

The 1920s capped Youngstown's building boom and brought more skyscrapers and new structures to Central Square. The Realty Building, opening in 1925, was the first of a quartet of buildings to rise on Central Square during the latter half of the 1920s. In 1926, the Keith-Albee (Palace)

The "Maid of the Mist" occupied the north island of the square from 1906 until 1923. *Courtesy of the author.*

Flag-raising with thirty thousand people gathered on the square, circa 1917. *Courtesy of the National Archives and Records Administration.*

Theater opened on the site of the former Second National Bank. The First National Bank Building also opened in 1926, and the Central Savings and Loan Building opened next to the square in 1929. "Very few cities with a square the size of this one can boast so many skyscrapers so close in proximity to the center point of the city," the *Vindicator* exclaimed.

In 1924, the old Diamond business block was torn down to make way for McCrory's five-and-dime store. This eroded the popularity of the Diamond nickname for the square, which the local government had originally tried to eliminate in an 1882 ordinance by declaring that the center of the city be called Central Square. With the disappearance of old haunts such as Diamond Hall—a popular ballroom that also hosted many touring speakers over the years, including temperance organizer Carrie Nation—the name gradually faded from the local lexicon.

The very heart of Central Square changed radically in the 1920s and '30s. In 1923, a small branch of the public library replaced the Maid of the Mist, which had been troubled by everything from pressure problems to drunks routinely falling into its waters. The city began removing the shade trees as well, a process that began during the administration of Joseph Heffernan in the early years of the Great Depression. An even more controversial development occurred during the Heffernan administration in 1931. After a raucous demonstration by communists, a common occurrence in the city in those years of extreme economic hardship, the mayor ordered a ban on any future oratory on Central Square. "Heffernan's order—if it stands threatened attack—means the end of the city's long famous public forum," remarked a *Vindicator* editorial.

For decades, the square had functioned as a kind of speakers' corner. Presidential candidates, perhaps most famously populist firebrand William Jennings Bryan (who orated from a makeshift platform in front of the Howell's Block), spoke on the square. And temperance advocates, labor organizers and all variety of cranks harangued crowds on the same grounds over the years. When courts upheld the ban, it proved to be another departure from Central Square's old role as a public space, a fact that seemed to disturb a good many Youngstowners, according to the *Vindicator*. The court's justification for upholding the ban was that Central Square, while formerly an ideal gathering place when Youngstown was a township, now proved too crowded by traffic flows to serve such a purpose anymore. This justification proved to be prescient. Over the next several decades, Central Square—and the downtown itself—would be increasingly treated as a place where automobiles (moving traffic, creating parking, etc.) dominated many aspects of city planning.

As early as 1919, editorials in the *Vindicator* and the *Youngstown Telegram* called for a radical reordering of the square to privilege traffic flows. The Youngstown Chamber of Commerce advocated for the removal of the Man on the Monument and the fountain, because they both "obstructed traffic." The chamber advanced a plan—according to journalist Paul Bellamy, who wrote about it for a *Plain Dealer* series on Ohio cities—calling for reducing the square islands to "a smooth strip of pavement" to expedite traffic flow. Another plan submitted to the chamber's "Public Square Committee" by architect Louis Miller called for a subway system, which would move northbound and southbound cars under Central Square. Ultimately, nothing became of any of these or similar proposals in the 1920s.

By the early 1920s, approximately eighty streetcars operated on eleven routes in the city. Gas motor busses were already present in Youngstown, as were about 135 privately owned touring cars known as jitneys, named after a slang term for the average fare, five cents. At the end of 1936, facing rising costs partly brought on by the Great Depression, the streetcar began

The southwest corner of Central Square as it appeared during the 1920s. *Courtesy of Thomas Molocea.*

to end, and the old trollies were replaced by trolley-busses in the late 1930s. In 1940, a new bus service replaced the last city rail line in Campbell. (Only the Youngstown and Suburban line remained, at least until 1948, when, according to *Motor Coach Age*, it was the last of the old operating interurban lines in Ohio.)

Buses took plenty of fares as the war era began. For most, motoring became more difficult due to wartime gasoline and tire rationing, along with the fact that practically no cars were produced from 1942 until the end of the war in 1945. According to the authors of *Mahoning Memories*, "By 1943 tires were in such severe shortage that buses of the Youngstown Municipal Railway Company strained to accommodate riders who left their autos in the garage." The popularity of the automobile, however, did not die during the Depression or war years. "The automobile remained an irresistible part of American life," writes urbanist James Howard Kunstler.

The city's population peaked in 1930, but growth in Mahoning County suburbs increased in the postwar era, a process made possible by the automobile. After the war, increasing amounts of car traffic poured

Auto traffic, public transit and pedestrians flow through the square in Depression-era Youngstown. *Courtesy of Thomas Molocea.*

downtown through Central Square. In response, the city fathers finally hoped to advance new plans for the old Diamond that had been put on hold by the Depression and the war. In 1947, the Youngstown Chamber of Commerce introduced a new plan to "streamline" the square. Proponents of the plan produced a copy of the original Youngstown plat of 1802 and pointed out that Central Square was originally an intersection with no islands. They argued for returning to the spirit of the original square.

Charles Owsley, chairman of the chamber's public improvements committee, proposed moving traffic straight through the square by eliminating the half-moon-shaped islands. This, of course, necessitated the removal of the Civil War Soldiers Monument. "A better home can be found for the Man on the Monument," a *Vindicator* editorial announced. "A more dignified and certainly more beautiful place for him can easily be made in Wick Park. Then the Public Square could be opened so that north–south and east–west traffic could move in a straight line instead of having to go halfway around the present circle." In short, the needs of motorists called for the end of the public part of Public Square. The chamber's plan required the complete elimination of the islands and an increase of parking space in the square by 83 percent.

The public and special interests soon weighed in on the proposal, delaying any action. By 1954, Youngstown planning director Israel Stollman had drafted another proposal. According to the plan, left turns would be allowed for north- and southbound vehicles, but not right turns. The islands would be trimmed, but not (as in the chamber plan) eliminated entirely. The Man on the Monument would still be moved. Due to the planned reduction of the north island, the Central Square Library was indeed closed and moved off the square in 1954. However, a public campaign to preserve the monument downtown by veterans and their wives gathered steam.

The *Vindicator* once again argued that, much like the city of Dayton—where the Civil War Soldiers Monument was moved off Main Street in 1948 to relieve traffic congestion—Youngstown should finally move its monument to Wick Park. Another 1954 *Vindicator* editorial argued that since the south island would no longer be completely eliminated, "wishes of the most deeply interested, the veterans, should be the governing factor." Postwar patriotism being what it was, the city ultimately decided to preserve the monument in the same spot it had occupied since 1870.

By 1960, downtown Youngstown, like many central business districts across the country in the postwar era, looked to be in decline. In 1955, Westminster Presbyterian Church, long a centerpiece of Central Square, began the process of decamping to Boardman. In the late 1950s, the Youngstown Sheet and Tube Company moved its corporate headquarters from the Stambaugh Building on the square to a new campus in Boardman. In 1951, the Greater Boardman Plaza opened. For the first time, suburban consumers (nearly 30 percent of consumer spending nationally came from suburban families in 1953) had a nearby shopping center located away from downtown Youngstown. The eventual opening of the Liberty Plaza in Liberty Township, along with the Wedgewood Plaza in Austintown, gave shoppers in the outlying townships alternatives to downtown stores.

According to the city planning commission, approximately 10 percent of the city's population worked downtown in 1960. The central business district occupied a fraction of 1 percent of the city's total land, but it represented 8 percent of the city's appraised value, the commission estimated. Downtown's position, however, was threatened. According to a city planning commission report from 1963, the central business district accounted for one-third less total sales in 1958 than in 1948. The planning commission recommended major changes to downtown, including many involving traffic problems. However, the report also gave attention to pedestrians, whom planners referred to as the "forgotten" element of downtown stability. Among other things, the report suggested that narrow side streets could be transformed into a pedestrian mall, prefiguring the

Central Square as it appeared on the eve of the urban renewal era, circa 1961. *Courtesy of Mark Peyko.*

next evolution of the downtown. As for Central Square, despite being the only designated public space downtown, planners described it as "so clogged with traffic and barren that it is seldom used by the public except as a place to review parades or solicit contributions to a charitable drive." The idea of Central Square as a public space had truly died.

The 1960s also witnessed the demolition of longtime landmarks downtown, especially on the square. This included the loss of the Palace Theater in 1966 and the Tod Hotel in 1969, both of which had dramatically altered the look and feel of the area. The Palace to the north, and the Tod to the south, helped frame the square and give it the appearance of an outdoor room. "I think that when you had the Palace Theater there and the Tod Hotel, you really had a strong sense of place," said local historian Mark Peyko. "There were these walls that contained you when you were in the square; it was a defined edge. When you lost the Palace Theater, you really lost that 'wall.'"

The space on the square where the Palace Theater once stood remains a parking lot today, but that is certainly not what developer Stephen Baytos advertised for the site back in the 1960s. A builder of shopping malls across the nation, he built the Legal Arts Center on the site of the former downtown Sears-Roebuck on Market Street in 1965 and the nearby Voyager Motor Inn in 1963. When the Palace closed in 1964, Baytos announced that the jewel of Central Square would be torn down to make way for a new project he dubbed "Plaza I." An eight-story building containing a mall and apartments would occupy the site of the former Palace Theater and Palace Hotel and would include a 1,200-seat Cinerama Theater called the "New" Palace Theater. Mayor Anthony B. Flask described the Legal Arts Center and the proposed Plaza I project to the *Vindicator* as "the most startling development in the city in fifty years." In 1966, Baytos announced his intention to acquire properties along East Federal Street and North Champion to build a department store, which would connect to the mall.

The Legal Arts Center did get built, though it did not meet the architectural quality evident in previous eras of buildings on Market Street. After the demolition of the Palace Theater, however, the much-hyped Plaza I and adjoining department store never materialized. In 1970, Lester Weinberg, a partner of the Dale-Howe Corporation, announced that a seventeen-story building (containing both office space and a "motor inn") would rise on the spot of the former Palace. An adjoining seven-story parking deck and social center were to accompany the new complex. The project was dubbed "People's Square," after Peoples Bank, which bought the property in 1969 and planned to have office space in the new complex. In 1972, the site of the proposed development was moved to the location of the former Tod Hotel. Nevertheless, the plans for the promised hotel and office space ultimately proved to be as illusory as the ill-fated Plaza I project. In 1980, the International Towers apartments were built on the former Tod property.

As the drama surrounding the Palace and Tod sites played out in the late 1960s and early 1970s, the city planned something of its own for the square: an effort to deliver on the proposed pedestrian mall concept mentioned in the planning commission report of 1960. Yet the actual mall that opened to the public in 1974 diverged from ideas put forward in the original proposals for "modernizing" the square. All the early proposals, according to Edmund Salata, deputy director of public works and city engineer in the early 1970s, involved depressing Wick Avenue and Market Street going through Central Square to fifteen or sixteen feet below grade.

One of the plans, proposed in 1965–66 and designed by Crane and Gorwic Associates, involved a pedestrian mall and plaza built over the depressed Wick-Market roadway. Escalators would bring shoppers from the parking lot below ground to the plaza above. Two northbound and southbound lanes would go under the square. East–west traffic on Federal Street would be prohibited at the square. The islands would be removed, and an ornamental pool with a fountain would replace the Man on the Monument, which the county proposed to relocate to the courthouse. Trees and planters would fill the rest of the square. After the election of Mayor Jack Hunter in 1969, the city scrapped plans to have a grade separation at Federal Street and Wick and Market, as cost estimates had jumped from $1.7 million to north of $3.0 million. Additionally, banks located on the square had basements extending underneath the sidewalks, and these would have been affected by the buildout.

According to the *Vindicator*, one of the reasons planners settled on the grade separation was a desire to implement "radical change" in the downtown business district. By the late 1960s, central business districts across the country were in marked decline. The continued movement of families to the suburbs, the rise of plaza shopping and enclosed shopping malls, along with the building of the interstate highway system, all shifted commerce away from downtowns and helped decentralize metropolitan areas.

One of the more radical solutions to urban decline, which older industrial cities pursued, was urban renewal. With help from the federal government, Youngstown demolished older urban neighborhoods to make way for redevelopment, light industry and the construction of the I-680 beltway around the city. City planners targeted urban renewal programs at the central business district as well, which led to the acquisition and demolition of almost all the commercial structures on East Federal Street in the late 1960s and early 1970s. As the city cleared the old business district on the east end of downtown in the early 1970s, work finally began on the complete transformation of Central Square. Following the lead of cities across the country, the city finally approved the creation of a pedestrian mall for the center of downtown called Federal Plaza, a name that replaced the old Central Square moniker.

As in other previous plans, east–west traffic on Federal was prohibited, but pedestrians could cross the Wick-Market throughway. The city reduced and elongated the square islands, providing traffic a more direct passage through the square. Traffic was also prohibited one block west of Wick Avenue and two blocks on the east. These sections were mostly covered in brick and landscaped. Thirty-eight-foot-diameter fountains greeted shoppers at both the east and west ends of the plaza. Also on the east end, a sunken amphitheater provided a venue for bands, shows and other forms

Federal Plaza under construction. *Courtesy of Silverio Caggiano.*

of entertainment. The fountains, as well as the walkable nature of the plaza itself, proved to be an attempt to compete with the growing popularity of the nearby enclosed malls of Eastwood and Southern Park, which opened in 1969 and 1970, respectively. The *Vindicator* stressed that Federal Plaza served "to provide a gravitational pull on shoppers, through the creation of an atmosphere of leisure, visual attractions and mostly vehicle-free surroundings."

Federal Plaza officially debuted to the public in the fall of 1974. At the dedication ceremony, Ohio Department of Transportation director J. Phillip Richley contrasted what he described as the dirty and poorly thought-out Central Square of the past with the new pedestrian-friendly plaza. To Richley, the mall provided a new start for the old square and for downtown: "The public square has gone public and has returned to the people with fountains and pools filled with water moving and reflecting, clusters of functional but decorative lighting, stone brick and masonry, flowers and trees and benches."

There was even an effort to open a four-hundred-seat theater inside Plaza Place, a brutalist structure erected off the plaza in 1975. "Plaza Palace" was one of the prospective names for the new venture. The brainchild of Richard Mills, the theater planned to screen first-run films, just as in nearby Pittsburgh and Cleveland. Scheduled to open in 1978, it would have been the first theater to operate downtown since the Paramount closed at the end of 1975. "It just doesn't make sense that a city this size doesn't have a downtown theater," Mills told the *Vindicator* in 1977. "I'm a strong believer in downtown. I think this theater is a natural extension of the Plaza Place complex." The theater, however, never got off the ground.

Despite its novelty and aesthetic beauty, Federal Plaza never delivered the shot in the arm the downtown needed. "The plaza had really good landscaping, it was really well designed, and it was beautiful. Yet it choked off a lot of the vitality of downtown," Peyko recalled. Bill DeCicco, who worked as a consultant on urban renewal projects for the city, said the later extension of Federal Plaza proved problematic. "I think the modifications to Central Square were largely acceptable. What was really the controversy, and helped kill business to a degree, was when they blocked off Federal Street in front of Strouss' and two blocks to the east."

It may be largely forgotten today, but at the time, the plaza was hailed by many as a game changer for the downtown. That number included Harvard-trained urban planner William Brenner, who authored the 1976 study *Downtown and the University*. According to Brenner, Federal Plaza represented

Central Square looking north, 2021. *Photo by the author.*

"the most positive change in the downtown since the building boom of the 1920s." After the closing of the Youngstown Sheet and Tube Campbell Works in 1977, there were still those who thought downtown Youngstown could readily weather the economic storm, and some cited Federal Plaza as one of the reasons for optimism. When Senator John Glenn spoke at the dedication of the west extension of Federal Plaza in October 1978, he said, "It's an honor to be here today and see the evidence that Youngstown is moving forward."

Whatever forward motion Federal Plaza symbolized proved short-lived. "You had two blows for downtown: the opening of the malls in the late sixties and early seventies," DeCicco recalled. "The final blow was starting in seventy-seven; everything went to hell when the mills went down." Indeed, even without the collapse of the steel industry, it is doubtful that Federal Plaza would have become successful. Between 1959, when Kalamazoo, Michigan, became the first major city to close its downtown to traffic in favor of a pedestrian mall, and the early 1980s, over two hundred cities built pedestrian malls. According to design critic Alexandra Lange, by the dawn of the new century, less than two dozen remained. Youngstown's was not among the survivors; the city dismantled the plaza and opened up Federal Street again to traffic in 2005. "There was a public notice in the *Vindicator* that they were renaming it Central Square again," Peyko remembered.

In the years since the end of Federal Plaza, a nascent revitalization has taken hold in downtown Youngstown. Though no longer the commercial center of Mahoning County, the old central business district still has a major role to play in efforts to stabilize the city. And at the core of downtown is still Central Square, which continues to carry symbolic weight in the history of the area. "We will never escape Central Square, that's for sure," Lawson emphasized. "It would not only be shortsighted but also tragic if it lost its meaning."

II

CENTRAL SQUARE LIBRARY MET NEEDS

OF GROWING CITY

For decades, the remains of a formerly iconic structure from Youngstown's Central Square sat decaying off Route 422 in Girard. For those of a certain generation, it would have been instantly recognizable. The roof was long gone, and the windows were boarded shut. Only two sculptured tiles, each depicting an open book next to a lamp of knowledge, gave any indication to the uninitiated as to the building's onetime use. The small structure served Youngstown as the Central Square Library for over thirty years. The concept emerged from the Progressive Era, a period in American history that witnessed numerous reforms in education and culture, among many other things. The little library itself was the brainchild of Joseph Wheeler, a distinguished graduate of the New York State Library School in Albany.

Wheeler was appointed acting librarian in 1915. In 1916, he helped open an early branch library inside the arcade of the Hippodrome Theater, a popular downtown vaudeville house. The small library consisted of two double bookcases behind glass doors. The station remained open from 9:00 a.m. to 9:00 p.m. and attracted numerous patrons coming from the evening vaudeville shows. When Harry Houdini performed at the Hippodrome, he gifted a copy of his book *The Unmasking of Robert-Houdin* to the library. Houdini browsed through the books in the arcade and complimented the library on having opened a branch at the theater, the *Vindicator* reported. The main library delivered new books daily to replenish the small library's shelves, which had room for 1,200 titles. By

1919, demand at the Hippodrome Branch had grown too large for the arcade to accommodate any further growth. Wheeler soon struck a deal with the Youngstown Municipal Railway Company to use a portion of a sheet-steel waiting station, built to shelter patrons waiting for the trolley, to house a small Central Square Branch. Dubbed the "Tin Library," it soon attracted a steady stream of patrons from around the "Diamond," as the center of downtown was often referred to in those days.

The library shelved approximately 3,500 books and was heated by a small stove. Trucks often made several trips a day to restock the branch's inventory. At its peak, circulation reached over 70,000 volumes a year. A special section of books about business and technology was a key feature of the new branch. Library officials estimated that as many as 700 books a day might be lent from the small building. In 1922, during a bid to "clean off the Square," Mayor George Oles called for the removal of the homely structure. The library reported in 1923 that 75,000 fewer books were circulated in the year after the closing of the branch.

Public outcry and Wheeler's redoubled efforts led to a new proposal to construct a library on Central Square in 1923. The library association proposed building a structure thirty-five feet in length on the site of the then nonfunctional "Maid of the Mist," a fountain located on the north side of the square. Two main reasons were advanced for building a new branch: to beautify the square, and to provide a more convenient location for workers to borrow books. Libraries were increasingly seen as tools in the Americanization process as well. And many city leaders, infused with ideals from the Progressive Era, now encouraged laborers to educate themselves. "The big [main] library building frightens some people away, especially foreign-born people, or working men in their overalls, who have a perfect right to use books but are afraid to ask for them," said Herman Ritter, chairman of the Retail Board of the Chamber of Commerce. "These are the people who should be encouraged to read, for they are full of ambition that we can well use in the development of Youngstown."

Wheeler defended his project by claiming the new branch would save workers valuable commute time. "The people won't come up on the hill," he explained, referring to the distance to the main library from Central Square. "It isn't because they don't want to. Most everybody here works and losing half or three-quarters of an hour on their way home to go up to Rayen Avenue to select a book is a big item in a worker's day." Politicians and some other prominent businessmen emphasized different reasons for approving the project. "My chief reason for approving the plan, however, is the greatly

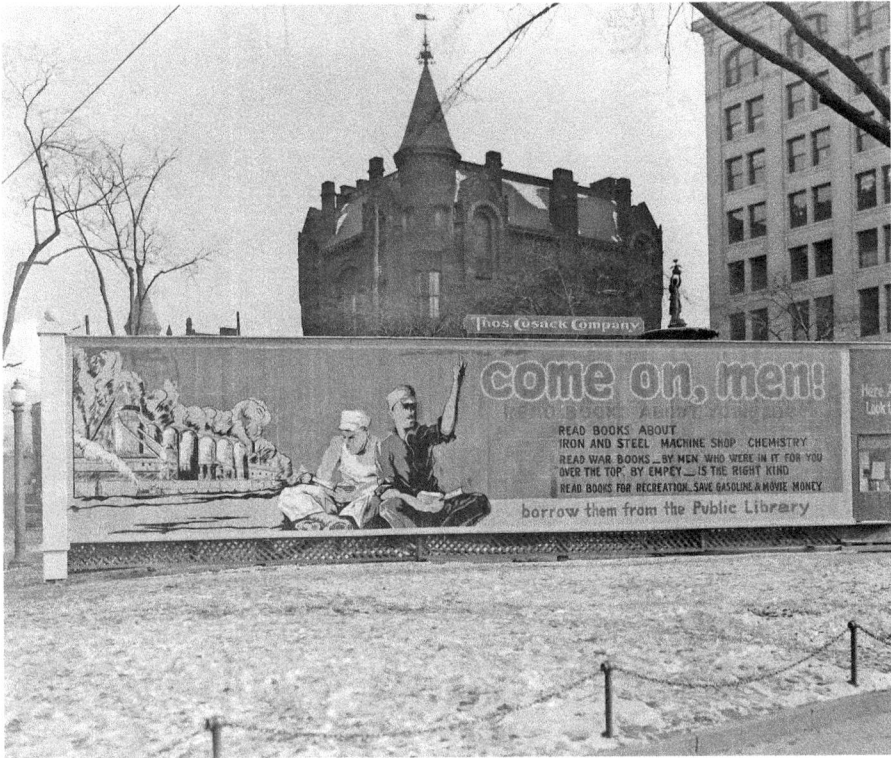

A public service announcement encourages workers to visit the Central Square branch of the library. *Courtesy of the Public Library of Youngstown and Mahoning County.*

improved appearance it will give the Diamond," former mayor Carroll Thornton exclaimed. A new library downtown would "serve to remind visitors that Youngstown is interested in books as well as dollars," said A.E. Adams, president of First National Bank.

Not everyone in the business community agreed. E.C. McMahon, the owner of a piano company on East Federal Street, opposed plans for the library, stating that Central Square should be reconstructed to reroute traffic more adequately through the center of downtown. He complained that the branch library would make that too difficult, thus hurting business on the east end of downtown. But such voices were in the minority, especially when library officials explained that the building could be constructed at no cost to taxpayers and was intended to be easily movable—in case planners sought to redesign Central Square in the future.

All materials and labor were donated by local contractors or paid for with donations, and work on the $10,000 structure began in the early fall

The Central Square branch was designed to mimic the architecture of the Butler Institute of American Art. *Courtesy of the Public Library of Youngstown and Mahoning County.*

of 1923. The green-tile roof and white-glazed terra-cotta building was meant to resemble the Butler Institute of American Art. The walls of the well-built precast shell were eighteen inches thick. The building's height was capped at fourteen feet to avoid blocking views from either the north or south.

Lights were placed under the eaves to broadly illuminate the library, which the *Youngstown Vindicator* soon described as "the outstanding feature of our public square." The lighting made the library highly visible at night without obscuring its architectural details. The branch formally opened on December 8, 1923, and held five thousand volumes. Like the old Tin Library, most of the books covered technical subjects, business and other works of nonfiction. However, the branch also offered works of fiction, especially the "classics." Patrons could reserve books from the main library and have them sent to Central Square as part of two daily deliveries. Like the former Hippodrome Branch, it operated from 9:00 a.m. to 9:00 p.m., six days a week.

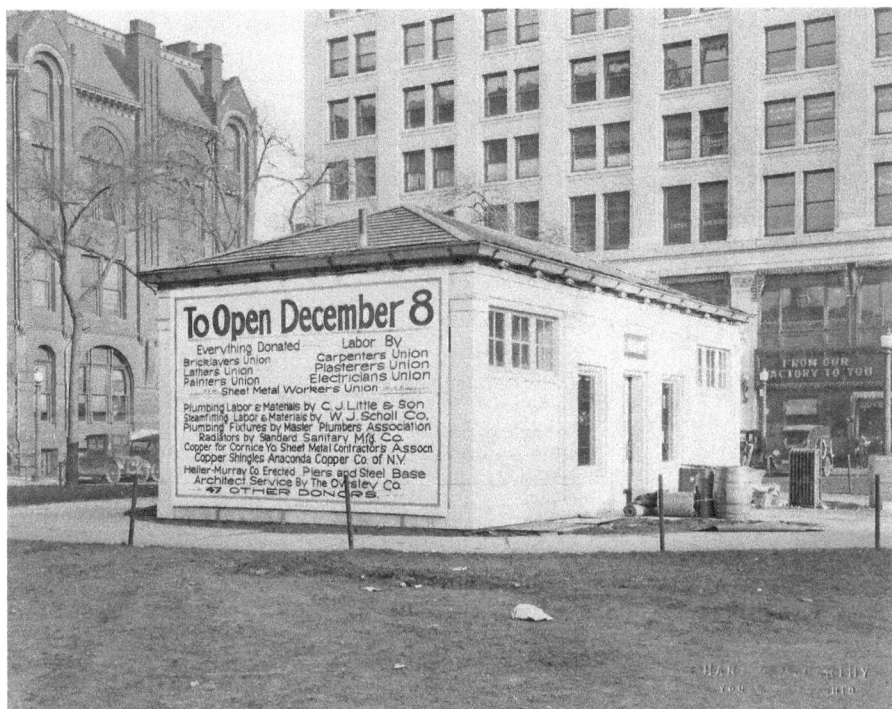

A banner on the rear of the library thanks those who contributed to the building's construction. *Courtesy of the Public Library of Youngstown and Mahoning County.*

The branch boomed along with downtown during the Roaring Twenties. At that time, much of retail and civic life centered on the central business district. "All the lodges and clubs were downtown," Youngstown resident Edward Manning later recalled. "The doctors, dentists and lawyers were all downtown. A good many of the churches were on Wood Street and in the downtown section."

The opening of more branches throughout the city, especially the opening of the new South Side Library in 1929, affected circulation at the Central Square Branch. However, its numbers soon rebounded and continued to grow—even during the height of the Great Depression. In 1939, circulation numbers at Central Square were higher than at any other branch in the county, with the exceptions of the Struthers and South Side Libraries. Mechanical books, heavily featured at the Central Square Branch, led in circulation during the latter part of the Great Depression. Books on foreign countries where American troops were stationed during World War II proved popular in the 1940s, according to library reports.

Library patrons at the circulation desk in an undated image. *Courtesy of the Public Library of Youngstown and Mahoning County.*

Interior of the library in an undated image. *Courtesy of the Public Library of Youngstown and Mahoning County.*

By the early 1950s, the city once again began discussing the possible reconfiguration of Central Square. Proposals were put forward to move both the library and the much-beloved Civil War memorial, known popularly as the "Man on the Monument," from the islands downtown. Keeping Central Square beautiful now took a back seat to the need to ease traffic congestion downtown. In 1953, a precipitous drop in funding for the library system and a decline in circulation of 1,463 books at the Central Square Branch caused the eventual closing of the library in 1954. Throughout its life, the little library circulated more than 2,000,000 books.

The building was sold to Boccia Construction and Demolition Company of Niles, and after three decades, one of the public library's most successful experiments came to an end. Countless workers and newly arrived immigrants were exposed to new worlds through the literature distributed by the Central Square Library. And though almost forgotten today, the little library on the square played an important role in the cultural evolution of the city.

12

When *Route 66* Rolled through
the Mahoning Valley

Youngstowners of a certain age may recall the scene: George Maharis and Martin Milner, stars of the TV show *Route 66*, are cruising in a Chevrolet Corvette convertible down Poland Avenue past miles of steel mills that once lined that route. "You know, Youngstown is not exactly on our course," Milner says in the opening minutes of the program. Youngstown is over one thousand miles from the legendary highway Route 66, but for a few days in May 1961, the cast and crew of the popular show filmed an episode titled "The Opponent" in and around the city. Many of the filming locations are long gone or changed beyond recognition. However, watching the episode opens a window into the grittiness and the urban character of the city in the early 1960s. It captured a now-vanished Youngstown as it appeared just before urban renewal and mass suburbanization—much as the show captured the atmosphere of American life as it transitioned from the 1950s to the 1960s. This is a rare glimpse behind the real-life locations used in the show.

At the time, Route 66 was the most famous stretch of road in the country. Nat King Cole recorded perhaps the most memorable version of "(Get Your Kicks on) Route 66," which summed up the place the "Mother Road" occupied in the American imagination: "If you ever plan to motor west / Travel my way, take the highway that is best. / Get your kicks on route sixty-six." *Route 66* aired on CBS from 1960 to 1964. Most of the show's 116 episodes, however, took place elsewhere. As the central actors, Maharis and Milner played two clean-cut drifters who moved from town to town, working odd jobs and falling into various adventures. "It was very, very interesting," Maharis later said of his experience on the show, "because no matter where you went, every town had its own personality. It was totally different from the other town you went to, even if it was only 50 to 60 miles away. That's not true anymore. You can go a 1,000 miles now, and everyone's wearing the same clothes, singing the same songs, eating the same food."

Youngstown's personality as a steel town, and especially in this case as a boxing town, led the show to film in the city. "In the '30s and '40s Youngstown was always associated in the minds of boxing enthusiasts as a great fight town," said Roger Leonard, administrative assistant to the producer. "Hundreds of good fighters have come from Youngstown, and that is why we figured this would be the perfect spot to do a fight story." The episode follows the duo as they seek out a once-great boxer turned palooka, Johnny Copa, played by Darren McGavin. As the opening credits roll, they drive northwest on Poland Avenue past the Campbell Works (where the Youngstown Sheet & Tube sign is clearly visible) and Republic Steel, turning right by the Castle restaurant. They make a stop at an auditorium where Copa later squares off against a Youngstown fighter. The auditorium and final fight scenes were filmed at the Struthers Field House.

Maharis and Milner are next seen walking past Central Square to East Federal Street as it existed before urban renewal. There are several amusing segments when extras stare and turn their heads as the actors walk by. You can see one extra pull another out of the way as the duo walks by. That would have never happened in Hollywood, but it gives a good indication of what might have happened in the many midwestern towns and cities where the show was filmed. Maharis told a WKBN reporter before filming began on East Federal, "When you do it [film] out in Hollywood, who comes out to meet you with a camera and a microphone? We're big wheels out here." At the time, *Route 66* was one of the few shows to film on the road.

In Youngstown, the pair discovers McGavin's character, Copa, and Scully, his trainer (Ed Asner), on the outskirts of downtown at what is called the Crown Hotel in the show. This was the Earle Hotel, a small establishment at the corner of West Federal Street and Belmont Avenue. The interior shots, however, were not filmed in the Earle. Views from the inside of McGavin's room reveal the Harshman and Ohio One buildings in the background, marking the Tod Hotel as the location of the interior shots. "I've never been in this town before," the broken-down boxer tells them as he looks out the window. "Scully says at night the sky is all lit up.

Central Square looking east at the time of the filming of the *Route 66* episode "The Opponent." *Courtesy of Mark Peyko.*

The shadows and the clouds, he says it's from the steel mills. He says the clouds act like mirrors, ya know?"

Copa's girlfriend (Lois Nettleton) follows him from city to city. She takes a job as a waitress at "the hottest club in town," called the Red Pony in the show, which is the Alibi Cocktail Lounge, formerly on Boardman Street next to the Hotel Pick-Ohio. Copa visits her there during a party for the Youngstown fighter (billed as "the pride of the Langden Steel Corporation") he is set to face in the ring. While Copa walks into the Alibi Lounge, Milner and Maharis confront local gamblers over a bet on the fight in a smoky poolroom. According to the *Vindicator*, the scene was filmed on West Federal Street, which makes Federal Billiards the most likely location.

During filming, the cast and crew stayed at the Congress Inn Motel on Market Street near North Lima. Maharis and Milner bought clothes from Squire Shop downtown, according to former employee Linda Rosenzweig Levine. They even found time, along with McGavin, to award the title of "Miss Youngstown" to Nancy Jean Lancaster of Struthers. Lancaster posed for photos with the three actors during a ceremony in the main ballroom at the Hotel Pick-Ohio.

After shooting on "The Opponent" wrapped, Maharis and Milner flew to Hollywood to attend the Emmy Awards, but they were not finished in

The interior scenes in the fictional Crown Hotel were filmed inside the Tod Hotel. *Courtesy of Mark Peyko.*

the Mahoning Valley. They returned the next week to begin filming a new episode. "We have a job in Kinsman," Maharis's character says during "The Opponent," and filming for the episode "Welcome to Amity" began in mid-May. Peck Prior, one of the show's agency men, had relatives in town and recommended Kinsman as a location, Roger Leonard said. "Prior convinced us that Kinsman would be the perfect spot."

In "Welcome to Amity," Kinsman is the setting for what appears to be an idyllic small Ohio town. When the episode begins, Maharis and Milner meet a mysterious young woman named Joan Maslow (Susan Oliver) at a boardinghouse. The octagonal home used for the boardinghouse is the childhood home of Clarence Darrow, which is in the National Register of Historic Places. Maslow spends the show on a quest to have her mother, who died a decade earlier, exhumed from a potter's field and reburied in the local Amity Cemetery, which is the Kinsman Cemetery. The boys are perplexed at the town's reaction to her decision. Everyone she meets is set on stopping her (sometimes violently) from moving her mother's body. When

Maslow's aunt attempts to legally prevent the disinterment of the body, the boys become determined to learn the secret that everyone in town seems bent on keeping from them.

The show alludes to the fact that the woman's mother engaged in numerous affairs and died in a drunken fall from a window while in the company of a married man, who turns out to be the boy's boss at the local foundry (the former Glauber Brass, which also appears in the show). According to the Kinsman Historical Society, the controversial nature of the episode caused the show to substitute the name *Amity* for *Kinsman*. In a 2007 interview, Maharis mentioned that the scripts were often finished at the very last moment. This could explain why Kinsman is mentioned by name in "The Opponent" but becomes Amity when filming began in Trumbull County.

The names of towns and cities were not regularly changed for the show. *Route 66* was filmed in Northeast Ohio for a month in 1961, and other shooting locations regularly made their way into the scripts—including several episodes filmed in Cleveland. In "First-Class Mouliak," also filmed in Cleveland, a fresh-faced Robert Redford makes an early appearance. Milner and Maharis returned to the region in August 1961 as special guests at the All-American Soap Box Derby in Akron. The show's producer, Sam Manners, was a native son of Cleveland, something that undoubtedly influenced the show to film in so many locations in Northeast Ohio. Yet Youngstown's and the region's appearance in such a popular show reflected a time when the heart of industrial America still prospered, and the cities of the Buckeye State represented a thriving Middle America.

13

Youngstown's Original
Farm-to-Table Stand

The south side of Youngstown roared along with the exuberant decade of the 1920s. As thousands of people moved into that rapidly growing part of the city, the Pyatt Street Market was born. Every year, shoppers descended on the farmers market to inspect the colorful stalls piled high with seemingly endless rows of fruits and vegetables. Generations of Youngstowners grew up with parents who brought them to a bustling venue that had been transformed from a city dump into one of the busiest farmers markets in Northeast Ohio.

According to Joseph Butler's *History of Youngstown and the Mahoning Valley, Ohio*, a group of about 150 local growers known as the Growers Market Company started a farmers' market on East Woodland Avenue in the early 1900s. In April 1920, they purchased three acres of land on Pyatt Street, and this would eventually lead to the establishment of the Pyatt Street Market. It first opened around 1924 and initially operated year-round on Mondays, Wednesdays and Fridays from 1:00 p.m. to 10:00 p.m. It was centered at 66 Pyatt Street. The stalls and vendors extended past Lois Court to Erie Street and up Pyatt to Wayne Avenue. "In the summertime the Pyatt Street Market used to be so packed," Joseph Rohovsky told YSU's oral-history program in 1982. "And the traffic was so great you couldn't even walk on the street."

Along with other young children, Rohovsky earned pocket money by shelling peas and lima beans for vendors in the early 1940s. At the time, as many as two thousand shoppers a day came through the market. In those days, neighborhood grocers dominated much of the grocery business in the

The long-closed Pyatt Street Market as it appeared prior to a 2012 fire. *Photo by the author.*

city. Lacking the proper refrigeration to keep produce consistently fresh, owners regularly visited the market for fruits and vegetables. Housewives made up the other largest group of shoppers, according to a *Vindicator* report from the time.

Farmers from a fifty-mile radius routinely came to sell their wares. The market consisted of both an open-air section and a covered section where meats (including live chickens) and cheeses were sold. Shoemakers and vendors selling peanuts, popcorn and doughnuts all did business at Pyatt. Even an organ grinder with his monkey often arrived to entertain shoppers. Business usually peaked in September and October, when many housewives bought winter supplies for canning, according to Rohovsky. "The crowds are 'home-gown,' too," said Betty Lovell of the Junior League in 1955. "And every type is represented, from the elegant lady sporting slacks and a long cigarette holder, who sweeps up in her convertible, to the plainly-dressed, hard-working woman who walks over with her basket."

The rise of supermarkets during the 1950s and '60s began to hurt business at the Pyatt. According to *Mahoning Memories: A History of Youngstown and Mahoning County*, 70 percent of Youngstown's neighborhood grocery stores closed between the end of World War II and 1970. Many farmers left the business altogether. "General Motors came, and a lot of the farmers' children ended up working there," Bill Umbel recalled. "They could make more money than they could breaking their backs on a farm." In 1981, the owners of the market admitted that it was difficult to compete with large grocery chains that offered "loss leaders" at a rate that they could never compete with. Umbel and Youngstown Food Distributors took control of the market in the early 1980s. Daily attendance had declined to an average of between four hundred and five hundred people a day, Umbel told the *Vindicator*.

In the mid-1980s, he and his wife, Janet, bought an old diner next to the market and rechristened it the Pyatt Street Diner. It originally opened as a breakfast and lunch spot for employees of Youngstown Food Distributors. "We started out with just four booths, eleven bar stools and a table in the corner," he said. It was initially called "Youngstown's best kept dining secret" by *Speed of Sound* magazine. However, it quickly became a notable success. The diner was known for selling pasta on Wednesday, beef on Thursday, fish on Friday and pork and lamb on Saturday. "We turned a diner with casual attire into a place with a white tablecloth menu," Umbel explained. In 1989, *Ohio Magazine* gave the diner a star rating. "It was really nostalgic," said former patron Don Attenberger. "The kind of old-time diner you just don't see today."

Exterior of the former Pyatt Street Diner, one of the city's premier eateries in the 1980s and '90s. *Photo by the author.*

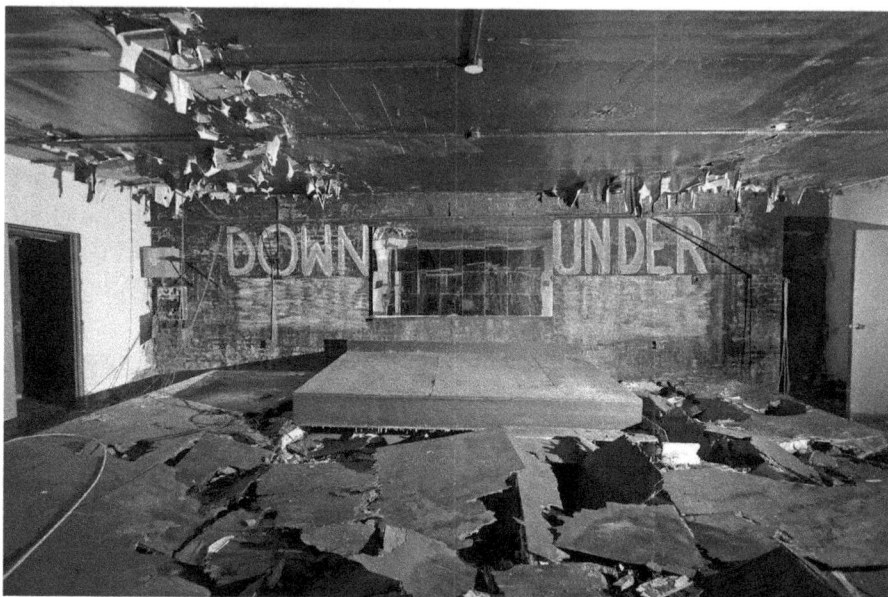

The abandoned Pyatt "Down Under" club. *Photo by the author.*

The Umbels also opened a club in the basement called "Down Under." *Speed of Sound* described it as "Youngstown's new jazz 'underground.'" It soon became a noted place to hear some of the best music the city had to offer. "Some of the biggest names in jazz and blues would come through," Umbel said. "They'd give us a decent price because it was an off night for them." Local acts like Big Boogie D and Youngstown native and world-class jazz musician Bill Kirchner thrilled audiences as well.

In 2000, the Umbels opened the Pyatt Street Diner II in Colony Square Plaza in Boardman. They wanted to provide a carryout option closer to the bulk of their clientele in the suburbs. Yet the old market on Pyatt Street continued to struggle as crime rose on the south side and younger customers failed to carry on the tradition of visiting farmers markets. "If I were a queen, I'd wave my magic wand and revive Youngstown's Pyatt Street Market," Jane Tims wrote in a 1998 *Vindicator* column. At one point, Architectural Incorporated of Boardman drew up plans for "Pyatt Street Market Square 2000," a new look for a new century. However, it was not to be. By 2004, both the market and the diner had closed. Only a few years later, the farm-to-table and farmers market movement arrived in the Mahoning Valley. If the Pyatt Street Market had survived until that point, could it have revived and still be functioning today?

A 2012 fire destroyed much of the covered section of the abandoned market, but, unbeknownst to many, there's still one reason to visit Pyatt Street today. Pam and Ken Krantz have been coming there now for almost forty years. They still operate their food truck, Kenny K's Concessions, under the old canopy on Monday, Wednesday and Friday from April to December. "We've seen four or five generations come through here," Ken said. For a few dollars, you can buy a hot sausage sandwich and French fries and hear about the glory days of the old market. While you wait, you're sure to see a diverse group of people pull up for the lunchtime rush. "They just come," Ken explained. "Just drive up Market Street and look down and see if we're here," Pam said. After almost a century, a small piece of Youngstown's longest-lasting farmers market still lives on.

14

CITY SKYLINE FOREVER ALTERED
BY ST. COLUMBA'S FIRE

For decades, the Gothic revival church of Saint Columba's remained a mainstay of the city's skyline. The impressive medieval-looking structure dominated Wood Street and the edge of downtown. From its dedication in 1903, it was perhaps the most beautiful and admired church edifice in the Mahoning Valley. And from 1943 until its untimely end by fire in 1954, it served as the first cathedral church of the Youngstown Diocese.

Well over a century before the creation of Dioecesis Youngstonensis, the early settlement started by John Young lacked any real opportunity for Catholic settlers such as Daniel Sheehy to partake in organized religious services, according to historian Thomas Welsh. "Few priests were active in America at the time, and large stretches of the Connecticut Western Reserve were bereft of the handful of missionary priests who helped sustain Catholic religious practices in other remote regions of the country." In about 1826, Reverend Thomas Martin traveled from Pennsylvania to celebrate mass for the first time in the Youngstown area at the home of William Woods, an in-law of Sheehy. In 1839, Youngstown Catholics received the services of a permanent pastor, Father James Conlon, who traveled from the St. Philip Neri Parish in Dungannon, the oldest in northeastern Ohio, to administer mass in private homes.

An 1847 meeting in William Woods's home set the stage for the organization of Youngstown Catholics into a mission parish with plans for the building of the area's first church. In 1853, a small wooden edifice emerged at the corner of Hazel and Wood Streets. The lumber for the church was cut and fashioned by the parishioners themselves. The mother parish was named for Saint Columba, an Irish monk renowned for his work in helping to convert Scotland to Christianity. In 1868, the second church, a more substantial brick building, opened on the hill above the Erie Railroad. The bricks for the church were brought by the male parishioners from a brickyard on Pike Street. It was years in the making, Margaret Murphy later told the *Youngstown Vindicator*. "They had a hard time building it," she said. "All the men of the parish helped. I remember that my husband would work his turn in the mill—and it was twelve hours— and then go up and help dig the cellar." The new parish thrived, even having its own publication with a monthly circulation of two thousand. The Catholic population of Youngstown grew as the nineteenth century progressed. According to the *Vindicator*, six parishes were direct offshoots of St. Columba's, including the oldest, St. Ann's, organized in 1869 in Brier Hill, then a village outside of Youngstown.

By 1893, construction was underway on what would be the third iteration of St. Columba's, located at the corner of West Wood and Elm Streets. In a stroke of ill-luck, the economic panic of that year put a halt to the new church's construction. The ensuing depression lasted for most of the decade and put a stop to any immediate hope of completing the edifice. Construction halted after the completion of the basement, which was covered and used as a parish hall until the building program resumed in 1900. The long-awaited dedication finally arrived with the appropriate pomp and circumstance in 1903. Over two thousand Catholics and non-Catholics alike attended the dedication ceremonies. Right Reverend Ignatius Frederick Horstmann, bishop of the Cleveland Diocese, presided over the ceremonies. According to the *Vindicator*, Horstmann declared that in all his years of traveling the country he had yet to see a more regal churchly edifice.

The new St. Columba's took its architectural inspiration from the Gothic churches that emerged all over France starting in the twelfth century. The imposing stone structure, built with granite from the Catskill Mountains, reflected the verticality typical of church design from that era, which was intended to give parishioners the feeling of being closer to God. Initially, two gray granite towers, extending toward the heavens, were among the most notable aspects of the design. In 1927, after pieces of the towers began crumbling, the stone shafts were cut down and two copper spires topped by crosses were erected. The towers took their inspiration from Norwich Cathedral in England. After this addition, the church extended ninety-eight

The neo-Gothic St. Columba's Church stood on Wood Street from 1903 until it was destroyed by fire in 1954. *Courtesy of Mark Peyko.*

feet from the street to the tops of the spires—equal to about nine stories in height. A beautiful rose window, one of the church's most notable flourishes, decorated the top of the main entrance. A decorative gable (two more graced the tops of the doors to the right and left) framed the archivolt and tympanum below.

The vestibule was finished in marble, as were the altars and the communion rail. A statue of St. Columba stood in the central niche. Four statues of guardian angels and representations of the Flight into Egypt and the Death of St. Joseph were nearby. Fourteen stations of the cross in relief work, which had been imported from Munich, depicted scenes in the life and passion of Christ. The floor of the sanctuary and the wainscoting were made of Italian marble. Statues of guardian angels were positioned at the end of the altar, and beneath was a carved scene of the Last Supper. A painting of the Crucifixion hung above the main altar. To the far left, stained-glass windows represented another scene of the crucifixion as well as the Coronation of Mary. The windows were done in two panels with tracery, typical of the Gothic style. The transept featured representations of everything from St. Columba to the Crucifixion and the Descent from the Cross.

The Hook and Hastings Company of Boston, the leading pipe organ maker of its time, crafted the church's organ, which was enclosed in a case of quartered oak decorated in green with gold leaf trim. In the early years, 1,500 light bulbs lit up the church's Gothic arches during special events. These were among the many fineries the church's interior offered. The church was 130 feet long from the inner door to the communion rail and 78 feet long from the widest point of the sanctuary. If the need arose, as it did during pontifical masses and other special events, St. Columba's could accommodate 1,600 parishioners.

The parish boundaries covered nearly twenty blocks in the dense confines of the city's north side and played host to the oldest parochial school in the area. The church itself was, according to Thomas Welsh, "described by locals as a 'fortress of faith,' a name that reflected (perhaps unconsciously) the defensive mentality prevalent among the White Catholic working classes at the time the building was completed in 1903." In some ways, St. Columba's stood as a symbol to Protestant reactionaries and some in the older Anglo communities who both hated and feared the recent Catholic arrivals. A 1914 *Vindicator* article described how those attitudes manifested themselves in conspiracy theories and rumors about how Catholics were "drilling for civil war" inside of St. Columba's or of a Catholic father's placing a gun inside the church's basement whenever a child was born, in preparation for religious war. Similar tales about Catholic servant girls plotting to assassinate their employers on the eve of election night in 1914 swirled around the city. Such anti-Catholic bigotry crystallized with the rise of a second iteration of the Ku Klux Klan, which also latched on to and gave such falsehoods new life during its rise to power in Youngstown and the Mahoning Valley in the 1920s.

In May 1919, St. Columba's was honored when Bishop John Patrick Farrelly formally consecrated the church. The bishop anointed the twelve interior crosses with myrrh and held a mass in a ceremony that lasted six hours. Father Edward Mears, pastor of the church for many years, found himself elevated to the rank of domestic prelate. He was the first in the city to receive such an honor, and as the *Vindicator* reported, "The event set a precedent in conferring that rank outside of cathedral cities." Monsignor Mears was also appointed dean of clergy of Mahoning, Columbiana and Trumbull Counties. St. Columba's rose to the status of irremovable rectorate. After the death of Mears in 1923, the Reverend Joseph Trainor assumed the pastorate of the church.

The church's ultimate honor arrived during the war years. In 1943, the Diocese of Youngstown was established, and St. Columba's was elevated to the status of cathedral church. The new diocese encompassed over three thousand square miles, containing the counties of Mahoning, Trumbull, Columbiana, Stark, Portage and Ashtabula. In July, the Reverend James McFadden was enthroned as the first bishop of the Youngstown See at a ceremony in the cathedral. Almost twenty bishops and archbishops, including Archbishop Edward Mooney of Detroit, attended. The sanctuary was enlarged and a throne for the bishop installed at the left side of the altar. A new altar made of Carrara, Verona and Escalette marble was installed later in 1943.

Several princes of the church pontificated at St. Columba's over the years, including Cardinal József Mindszenty of Hungary, Cardinal James McGuigan of Canada, and Cardinal Thomas Tien Ken-sin of China. Most famously, Cardinal Mooney conducted a pontifical mass at the church in 1946. A Maryland native, he had lived in Youngstown as a boy in the Irish neighborhood of Kilkenny off Poland Avenue. Mooney attended St. Columba's School on Franklin Avenue and became an altar boy at the church. His reception at the cathedral was described by the *Vindicator* as "medieval in its splendor." A capacity crowd (with hundreds more standing out in the street) strained to see the archbishop. Mooney exclaimed that Youngstown was still in his heart, and he paid tribute to the late Father Mears, whom Mooney had served under at St. Columba's. "I feel the spirit of the dead as well as the hearts of the living are with us today," he said. "He personified for that generation the faith of St. Columba's and the faith of Youngstown."

The church as it appeared after the addition of the twin copper spires. *Courtesy of Thomas Molocea.*

By the early 1950s, according to *Vindicator* columnist Esther Hamilton, the cathedral on Wood Street had been struck by lightning four times, including one memorable occasion during a service when a strike knocked stones off the old towers onto the street below. On the night of September 2, 1954, a severe storm settled over Youngstown, and sometime around 9:30 p.m., lightning struck the cathedral, causing a fire in the choir loft. Even though several residents in the area reported that they were "rocked" by the sound of the strike, it was not until nearly 11:00 p.m. when a passerby came to the rectory to report a fire and the alarm was finally tripped.

Eleven companies of firemen arrived, but Assistant Fire Chief Frank Quinn later said the fire was "completely out of control" when they arrived. Nevertheless, the fact that a string of high-voltage wires extended in front of the cathedral made it impossible for the companies to raise their aerial ladder to its full height, leaving them powerless to reach the fire. "At first it appeared that firemen had the blaze under control," the *Vindicator* reported, "but when the streams of water couldn't reach the loft of the cathedral flames spread across the roof toward the rear of the building." Extreme heat blew out the windows, and the rear steeple collapsed into the street in a fiery heap. Groups of onlookers prayed for God to save the steeples as the fire continued to spread. Others ran inside to save art, vestments and whatever else they could carry. Records were hastily removed from the rectory. It was ultimately saved along with the new school in the rear of the church. Flashes of lightning lit up the sky as the fire burned into the small hours of the morning. The embattled fire companies later told the *Vindicator* that it had been "the saddest fire we ever fought."

In the aftermath of the inferno, the city's building inspector condemned the gutted cathedral as unsafe. The scorched altars were falling apart from the heat. The stone facing and joints had cracked, and the walls still left standing were declared a hazard. The roof was gone, leaving St. Columba's in a state much like the ruined cathedrals of World War II–era Europe. Insurance covered $940,000 worth of losses, but the damage was estimated at $1,250,000, making it perhaps the costliest fire in city history.

Bishop Emmet M. Walsh, who had succeeded Bishop McFadden after his death in 1952, immediately began fundraising. However, not everyone in the community was content to mourn the church or contribute money to erecting a new one. According to Thomas Welsh, the question of why the city (after multiple requests to do so) had never removed the high-voltage wires from in front of the cathedral continued to persist after the fire. Initially, the wires were an eyesore, but now they appeared to have led to the cathedral's

The cathedral's interior lay in ruins after the calamitous fire of September 2, 1954. *Courtesy of Thomas Molocea.*

destruction. The subtext of questions like these likely had roots in what some may have thought of as the bygone era of strained relations between area Catholics and the old political establishment in Youngstown. This included the not-so-distant memory of the Klan and its allies in the city.

Consternation, particularly among older Catholics, continued with the building of a new cathedral. Planning had already begun in late 1954, and construction was finished in 1958. In a dedication booklet for the church's opening, the diocese declared St. Columba's thoroughly contemporary in both concept and design: "Replacing the Roman, Grecian, and Gothic styles so profusely borrowed until a generation ago, the new cathedral in its modern concept is not only an addition to contemporary ecclesiastical design but also a development in the field of American architecture. It is an example of the clean, uncluttered modern design adapted to sacred and dignified purpose."

For some parishioners, this was precisely the problem. The architectural style reflected a modernized Romanesque design, and the exterior masonry consisted of Mankato stone. Ornamentation was kept to a minimum. It could not have been further from the neo-Gothic style of the previous structure. Esther Hamilton wrote in a column that when the statue of St.

Columba was placed in front of the church (in keeping with the new church's simplicity of design, no other statues were present inside the cathedral), a woman standing in front of the church commented, "He's too fat." Another member of the congregation immediately told Father Glenn Holdbrook (who had succeeded Reverend Trainor after his death in 1956) that she hated the St. Columba statue. When the first High Mass at the new church was given in November 1958, Reverend Holdbrook addressed those who felt uncomfortable in the new modern cathedral. "No architect can design memories or build traditions," he said. "I can assure you this house of God will in its day fulfill its mission of memories."

Indeed, in the decades to come, new memories were made and milestones marked in the new cathedral. St. Columba's survived the era of urban renewal, which destroyed much of the surrounding neighborhood during the expansion of Youngstown State University, and the economic collapse of Youngstown in the wake of Black Monday. In 1997, when the parish celebrated its 150th anniversary, Reverend Lawrence Fye summed up the strength of St. Columba's and the Catholic tradition in Youngstown: "It still stands here as witness. One hundred fifty years in our society is a long time to be in existence and still be thriving."

BIBLIOGRAPHY

Books

Blevins, Rich. *Ed McKean: Slugging Shortstop of the Cleveland Spiders*. Jefferson, NC: McFarland & Company, 2014.

Blue, Frederick J., William D. Jenkins, William Lawson and Joan M. Reedy. *Mahoning Memories: A History of Youngstown and Mahoning County*. Virginia Beach, VA: Donning Company Publishers, 1995.

Boryczka, Raymond, and Lorin Lee Cary. *No Strength Without Union: An Illustrated History of Ohio Workers, 1803–1980*. Columbus: Ohio Historical Society, 1982.

Brody, David. *Labor in Crisis: The Steel Strike of 1919*. New York: J.B. Lippincott, 1965.

Brown, Ryan C. *Pittsburgh and the Great Steel Strike of 1919*. Charleston, SC: The History Press, 2019.

Bukowski, Douglas E. "Charles A. Comiskey: Baseball as American Pastime and Tragedy." In *The Human Tradition in Urban America*, edited by Roger Biles, 87–100. Wilmington, DE: Scholarly Resources, 2002.

Butler, Joseph, Jr. *History of Youngstown and the Mahoning Valley, Ohio*. Chicago: American Historical Society, 1921.

Cowie, Jefferson. *The Great Exception: The New Deal and the Limits of American Politics*. Princeton, NJ: Princeton University Press, 2016.

Fleitz, David L. "Jimmy McAleer." In Nowlin, *Opening Fenway Park with Style*, 183–87.

Foster, William Z. *The Great Steel Strike and Its Lessons.* New York: B.W. Huebsch Incorporated, 1920.

Galida, Florence. *Fascinating History of the City of Campbell.* State College, PA: Jostens American Yearbook Company, 1976.

Hagedorn, Ann. *Savage Peace: Hope and Fear in America, 1919.* New York: Simon & Schuster, 2007.

Hickey, Dennis, John Olszowka, Brian R. Sheridan and Marnie M. Sullivan. *America in the Thirties.* Syracuse, NY: Syracuse University Press, 2014.

Holbert, Craig, Margaret Maroon and Thomas Maroon. *Akron-Canton Baseball Heritage.* Charleston, SC: Arcadia Publishing, 2007.

Holway, John. *Voices from the Great Black Baseball Leagues.* Rev. ed. Mineola, NY: Dover Publications, 2010.

Interchurch World Movement of North America. *Report on the Steel Strike of 1919.* New York: Harcourt, Brace and Howe, 1920.

Jenkins, William D. *Steel Valley Klan: The Ku Klux Klan in Ohio's Mahoning Valley.* Kent, OH: Kent State University Press, 1990.

Jones, Nathaniel R. *Answering the Call: An Autobiography of the Modern Struggle to End Racial Discrimination in America.* New York: News Press, 2016.

Katz, Michael B. *In the Shadow of the Poorhouse: A Social History of Welfare in America.* New York: Basic Books, 1986.

Komisar, Lucy. *Down and Out in the USA: A History of Social Welfare.* New York: Franklin Watts, 1974.

Kunstler, James Howard. *The Geography of Nowhere: The Rise and Decline of America's Man-Made Landscape.* New York: Simon & Schuster, 1993.

Lammers, Craig. "Casey Hageman." In Nowlin, *Opening Fenway Park with Style*, 95–101.

Linkon, Sherry L., and John Russo. *Steeltown U.S.A.: Work and Memory in Youngstown, Ohio.* Lawrence: University of Kansas Press, 2002.

Melnick, John C. *The Green Cathedral: History of Mill Creek Park, Youngstown, Ohio.* Youngstown, OH: Youngstown Lithographing, 1976.

Mjagkij, Nina. *Light in the Darkness: African Americans and the YMCA, 1852–1946.* Lexington: University Press of Kentucky, 1994.

Nowlin, Bill, ed. *Opening Fenway Park with Style: The World Champion 1912 Boston Red Sox.* Phoenix, AZ: Society for American Baseball Research, 2012.

Peyko, Mark C. "Despite Apparent Benefits, WPA Program Was Fraught with Controversy." In *Remembering Youngstown: Tales from the Mahoning Valley*, edited by Mark C. Peyko, 48–53. Charleston, SC: The History Press, 2009.

Spinney, Laura. *Pale Rider: The Spanish Flu of 1918 and How It Changed the World.* New York: Public Affairs, 2017.

Stewart, Catherine A. *Long Past Slavery: Representing Race in the Federal Writers' Project*. Chapel Hill: University of North Carolina Press, 2016.

Strickler, David L. *Child of Moriah: A Biography of John D. "Bonesetter" Reese, 1855–1931*. Montrose, CO: Four Corners Press, 1984.

Taylor, Candacy. *Overground Railroad: The Green Book and the Roots of Black Travel in America*. New York: Abrams Press, 2020.

Taylor, Nick. *American-Made: The Enduring Legacy of the WPA: When FDR Put the Nation to Work*. New York: Bantam, 2008.

Turchin, Peter. *Ages of Discord: A Structural-Demographic Analysis of American History*. Chaplin, CT: Beresta, 2016.

Wilkerson, Isabel. *Caste: The Origins of Our Discontents*. New York: Random House, 2020.

Worth, Richard. *Baseball Team Names: A Worldwide Dictionary, 1869–2011*. Jefferson, NC: McFarland & Company, 2013.

Commissioned Reports

Community Research Associates of New York. *Social Welfare Consideration Involved in the Construction and Operation of the Mahoning County Home*. New York, 1960.

Genealogical Society Reports

Powers, William Tatnall. *Mahoning County, Ohio Infirmary Deaths*. Ohio Genealogical Society, 1994.

Simon, Margaret Miller. *Canfield Township Cemetery and Death Records, Mahoning County, Ohio*. Mahoning County Chapter of the Ohio Genealogical Society, 1983.

Troutman, Roger K. *Ohio Cemeteries, 1803–2003*. Ohio Genealogical Society, 2003.

Government Reports

The United States Conference of Mayors. *The Major Cities of the United States Report on the Relief Situation*. Washington, D.C., 1939.

Interviews with the Author

Stacey Adger, 2020.
Bennie Allison, 2019.
Don Attenberger, 2015.
Bill DeCicco, 2020.
Vince Guerrieri, 2020.
Shedrick Hobbs, 2015.
Ken Krantz, 2018.
Pam Krantz, 2018.
Bill Lawson, 2020.
Al Leonhart, 2020.
Theresa Lyons, 2019.
Mark Peyko, 2020.
Tim Sokoloff, 2021.
Barbara Stevens, 2019.
Bill Umbel, 2014.

Magazine and Journal Articles

Bear, B.M. "Youngstown." *Motor Coach Age* 22, no. 8 (1970): 4–15.

Business Digest. "Building Concrete Sectional Houses." August 14, 1918.

Christian, Mark. "Marcus Garvey and the Universal Negro Improvement Association (UNIA)—With Special Reference to the 'Lost' Parade in Columbus, Ohio, September 25, 1923." *Western Journal of Black Studies* 28, no. 3 (2004): 424–34.

DeBlasio, Donna. "'A Splendid Place to Live': Housing and the Youngstown Sheet and Tube Company." *International Journal of Regional and Local Studies* 3, no. 1 (2007): 30–55.

Engineering News-Record. "Unit-Built Concrete Cottages to House Foreign Labor." April 11, 1918.

Fitch, John A. "Arson and American Citizenship: East Youngstown and the Aliens Who Set the Fire." *Survey*, January 22, 1916.

Hatchett, Richard J., Carter E. Mecher and Mark Lipsitch. "Public Health Interventions and Epidemic Intensity During the 1918 Influenza Pandemic." *Proceedings of the National Academy of Sciences of the United States of America* 104, no. 18 (2007): 7582–87.

Herding, F.J. "Workingmen's Colony, East Youngstown." *American Architect* 114 (October 2, 1918): 383–98.

Kuegle, Paul C. "Industrial Housing." *Yearbook of the American Iron and Steel Institute* (1923): 107–15.

Salata, Edmund J. "Public/Private Support Brings This Downtown Back to Life." *American City*, March 1975.

Vorse, Mary Heaton. "Behind the Picket Line: The Story of a Slovak Steel Striker-How He Lives and Thinks." *Outlook*, January 21, 1920.

Whipple, Harvey. "146 Unit-Built Concrete Dwellings at Youngstown." *Concrete-Cement Age* 12, no. 2 (January 1918).

Newspapers

Chillicothe (OH) Gazette

Mahoning (OH) Dispatch

Mahoning (OH) Register

New York Times

Niles (OH) Daily Times

Plain Dealer (Cleveland, OH)

Republican Sentinel (Canfield, OH)

Toledo (OH) Blade

Washington Evening Star

Weekly Guernsey Times (Cambridge, OH)

Western Sentinel (Winston-Salem, NC)

Youngstown (OH) Telegram

Youngstown (OH) Vindicator

Online Resources

"Born in Slavery: Slave Narratives from the Federal Writers' Project, 1936–1938." http://memory.loc.gov/ammem/snhtml/.

"George Maharis Interview Reveals a Lot About Route 66 TV Drama." https://www.route66news.com/2007/10/15/a-chat-with-george-maharis.

Lauth, Wendell F., Jennifer L. Neff and Patricia D. Wiant. "The Mahoning County Infirmary: Canfield Township, Mahoning County, Ohio." The Pogy. https://www.thepogy.com.

Oral Histories

Armstrong, Herbert. Interview by Peter Chila. March 3, 1994. https://scholar.lib.vt.edu/faculty_archives/principalship/a/310armstrong.html.

Hendricks, Gertrude. Interview by Elisa Calabrese. December 9, 1985. Transcript. Westlake Terrace Project, O.H. 658. Youngstown State University Oral History Project, Youngstown, Ohio.

Higley, Joseph, Jr. Interview by Paul Carlson. April 15, 1977. Transcript. Youngstown Law School Graduates, O.H. 56. Youngstown State University Oral History Project, Youngstown, Ohio.

Kish, Billy. Interview by William M. Kish. July 15, 1989. Transcript. Campbell, Ohio, During the 1930s and 1940s, O.H. 1327. Youngstown State University Oral History Project, Youngstown, Ohio.

Manning, Edward C. Interview by D. Scott Van Horn. May 14, 1986. Transcript. Youngstown in the 1920s and 1930s, O.H. 666. Youngstown State University Oral History Project, Youngstown, Ohio.

Rohovsky, Joseph. Interview by Philip Bracy. December 17, 1982. Transcript. Life at Pyatt Street Market, O.H. 279. Youngstown State University Oral History Project, Youngstown, Ohio.

Ross, John. Interview by Philip Bracy. April 20, 1981. Transcript. Youngstown, (Campbell) 1916 Fire and Riot, O.H. 1052. Youngstown State University Oral History Project, Youngstown, Ohio.

State and Local Government Documents

Coordinating Council of the Community Corporation of Greater Youngstown. *Mahoning County Home: Present and Future.* Youngstown, Ohio, 1953.

Ohio General Assembly, House of Representatives. *Journal of the House of Representatives of the State of Ohio, Volume 65.* Columbus, Ohio, 1859.

Youngstown City Planning Commission. *Economic Analysis for the Central Business District, CPC Report No. 63-3, Central Area Report No. 4.* Youngstown, Ohio, 1963.

———. *Findings of the Downtown Inventory.* Youngstown, Ohio, 1960.

———. *Toward a Downtown Plan—Preliminary Planning Proposals.* Youngstown, Ohio, March 1960.

Unpublished Manuscripts

Beelen, George D. "The Negro in Youngstown: Growth of a Ghetto." Seminar paper, Kent State University, 1967.

Brenner, William A. *Downtown and the University: Youngstown, Ohio.* Youngstown, 1976.

Peyko, Mark C. "Understanding the Downtown." Master's thesis, Eastern Michigan University, 1991.

Schisler, Wade. "My Fond Memories of the Mahoning County Home." Canfield Historical Society.

Welsh, Thomas G. "Cross Purposes: Catholic Disunity and the Decline of Youngstown's Parochial Elementary Schools, 1964–2006." PhD diss., Kent State University, 2009.

INDEX

About the Author

S ean T. Posey is a freelance writer and historian. He holds a bachelor's degree in photojournalism from the Academy of Art University in San Francisco and a master's degree in history from Youngstown State University. His work has been featured in a variety of publications, including *Citylab*, *Salon* and *Bill Moyers and Company*, as well as in the books *Car Bombs to Cookie Tables: The Youngstown Anthology* and the *Pittsburgh Anthology*. The History Press also released Sean's first two books, *Lost Youngstown* and *Historic Theaters of Youngstown and the Mahoning Valley*.

Visit us at
www.historypress.com

www.ingramcontent.com/pod-product-compliance
Lightning Source LLC
Chambersburg PA
CBHW070354100426
42812CB00005B/1505